# Not Yet Sunset

## A Story of Survival and Perseverence
## in LRA Captivity

pray without
ceasing

Grace Acan

FOUNTAIN PUBLISHERS
www.fountainpublishers.co.ug

Fountain Publishers
P.O. Box 488
Kampala
E-mail: sales@fountainpublishers.co.ug
        publishing@fountainpublishers.co.ug
Website: www.fountainpublishers.co.ug

ISBN  978-9970-25-936-6

# Dedication

This book is dedicated to my beloved children Beatrice, Tresina and Josh, not forgetting Ogenrwot (RIP) who will forever be remembered even when you did not live with us for long. To my family and friends who never ceased praying till my return, and to each and everyone who made tireless efforts physically, socially, and emotionally to see that I am who I am today.

# Table of Contents

# Acknowledgement

I acknowledge Dr. Erin Baines and Ketty Anyeko for their countless support and guidance through out the entire process of writing this book. Thank you to the Justice and Reconciliation Project, the Social Science and Humanities Research Council, Dr. Pilar Riaño-Alcalá, Lindsay McClain Opiyo, Alison James, Aber Janet, Amony Evelyn and everyone whose name I have not mentioned here, for giving me all the necessary support in writing this book. Thanks to Fountain Publishers, and each member of their team for working tirelessly to see that this book is published. Above all, I am indebted to my family members, especially my parents, my siblings and my children for being there for me through out the writing process. May the almighty God bless you abundantly.

# Preface

On October 10th 1996, just past 1:00 am, 139 schoolgirls were abducted by the Lord's Resistance Army (LRA) from St. Mary's College in Aboke, which used to be in Apach but is presently Kole District in Uganda. The deputy headmistress Sister Rachelle Fassera followed the rebels into the night and upon catching up with them, pleaded for the girl's release. She was able to go back to the school with 109 girls, but 30 remained behind. Grace Acan was one of them. That night, she could not have imagined that she would eventually spend nine years in captivity period.

The war in northern Uganda began shortly after the current President, Yoweri Museveni, assumed office as the leader of the National Resistance Army (NRA) in 1986. As his rebel army deposed the national army, soldiers from the north fled their homes. It wasn't long before they reorganised into a resistance army themselves, seeking to protect their homeland from the arrival of the NRA. The rebellion quickly manifested as a spiritual movement – first under Alica Auma 'Lakwena' and later under a young Joseph Kony who remains the spiritual leader and chief commander of what became the Lord's Resistance Army (LRA). In 1994, the LRA secured the support of the Sudanese Government, and moved its bases to southern Sudan where it launched military operations and raids on civilian property. Tens of thousands of children and young persons were abducted and forced to carry looted goods to Sudan, where they were also trained as soldiers to fight in the army. Young women were forced to marry commanders and bear children, where Kony sought to create a 'new Acholi nation,' *Acholi MaNyen*. The LRA remained in Sudan until the early 2000s when it was finally rooted out by the Ugandan military, but re-entered Uganda and undertook a massive military campaign. A total of 1.7 million people were displaced into camps in north and eastern Uganda. The LRA escalated the rate at which children and adults were being abducted. The number had risen by tens of thousands by 2004. It was during this period that Grace escaped the LRA.

I first met Grace's mother, Consy Ogwal, at a prayer meeting held for children in Lira in 2003. When I learned that Consy's daughter had finally returned, I went to Lira to visit her and meet Grace in person. Although she had come out only a few weeks prior, Grace was already determined to return to school. I would visit her during the years following and a friendship developed. On holidays, Grace would join me where I worked at the Justice and Reconciliation Project in northern Uganda to help a young and growing team work with communities affected by violence, to document their experiences and develop strategies for seeking reparations, recognition and justice. Grace was keen to pick up on the justice issues they faced, particularly on questions of gender equality. When she graduated, she came on as a volunteer and eventually a Project Assistant to continue her passion to serve communities and work with women and children affected by war. During her studies, Grace read Ishmael Beah's book *A*

*Long Walk Home*, the memoir of a former child soldier from Sierra Leone, and was inspired. She began writing her own memoir at night after school and work, with the intention of releasing it for the world to get to know her experiences of life in the LRA. This was important to her, she once told me, because so many others had come to Uganda to write the story of the Aboke Girls, and didn't quite get it right.

The abduction of the Aboke girls has received a great degree of international attention and recognition following the tireless advocacy of the parents of the missing girls who had formed; The Concerned Parents Association (CPA). The story of Sister Rachelle and of mothers insisting on the safe return of their children in CPA, captured the hearts of everyone from the American television personality Oprah Winfrey to the Pope. The story of the Aboke girls became further known after Els DeTemmerman wrote *The Aboke Girls*, published by Fountain Publishers, and subsequently through journalists and writers in many other journal articles, books and documentaries. Within the LRA, this global attention fulfilled the prophecy of the spirits, which guided the group through its leader Joseph Kony, who had determined their abduction would 'make the LRA famous to the world'. It unfortunately also led to further segregation and discrimination of the girls by other captives, as Grace describes in painful detail.

This is a remarkable and courageous book. Grace takes us through the joys of childhood where she learned from her grandmother the value of being a Luo woman, an informal education that she feels helped her retain a sense of dignity in the LRA. She discusses her early school days where she first set her life goal of realising gender equality in her country, a theme that runs throughout her memoir and inspires her present work with communities affected by war. Grace captures in candid prose, the memories of the fateful day she was abducted, and the two months she spent inside the LRA group of Major Lagira evading the Ugandan military that hotly pursued the 30 Aboke Girls following international and national media attention to their abduction.

On arrival in Sudan where the rebels had established large military bases with as many as 5,000 people, Grace provides in vivid, tragic detail the struggles of daily life in the LRA. She reflects on the many ways she and the Aboke girls experienced intense discrimination within the LRA by other abducted persons and commanders alike, who questioned why the world continued to insist on their release, yet remained quiet about them. Segregated and alone within different high commanders' homes, she and her former classmates found few ways to communicate to each other and give each other hope of one day returning. Looking to the sky and seeing planes above, in poetic prose Grace states she always wished 'to catch the the wings of the aircraft passing by and fly away' from the camps. Her story explains starkly why this was a seemingly impossible task. Grace's dream of continuing her education and returning home never wavered, despite the ongoing hardship of life in Sudan.

Her story of escape is heart-wrenching as she labored to keep herself and her two children alive during the relentless fighting between the Ugandan military and rebels. Losing her son in a terrible bombing, she clung to life with her baby daughter and the hope of a better future for them. Surely today Grace is not only closer to that goal, but to realizing it for others as she shares her stories and courage to inspire the next generation of Ugandans. This book is a gift of words, heartache and hope, which she gives to Ugandans and the whole world as a challenge to work together for a future that recognises its past, and realises its dreams.

At the time of writing, the LRA still operates in the Democratic Republic of Congo, the Central African Republic and partly Sudan.


*Erin Baines*
Gulu, Northern Uganda
June 28, 2015

# 1

# Growing up in war

*"This is the story...of my experience during the war."*

My name is Grace Acan, and the Lord's Resistance Army (LRA) abducted me in the night from my dormitory at St. Mary's College Aboke. The date was October 10th, 1996. This is the story of my life before, during and after my abduction.

As a child, I studied in Holy Rosary Nursery School in Gulu, where I believe I was the happiest child. I felt everyone I met both at school and at home liked me. I remember my mother was working and could not pick me up from school at midday, so I would stay in school until 4 p.m when she was done with work. While waiting for her, I would be with the sisters in the convent. As my mum narrated to me, I was a very active girl. I remember one day, I did not want to wait in school until my mum came, as she always did. I just decided to leave and walk home by myself. I knew the way home, but one thing after another went wrong. It started raining when I had just reached town, so by the time I reached a bridge over a sewage channel, I was completely drenched to the skin. To make matters worse, the channel had flooded, and the bridge was not visible. So I stood stranded on one side shivering in the cold rain, as I watched people cross over a sewage pipe that was impossible for me to use.

Fortunately, Josephine, our family friend saw me, and carried me on her back to the other side and left me there. I was so grateful for the help she gave me, and she even assured me she was going to tell my mum to come to my rescue. In about ten minutes, I saw my mum coming. She carried me on her back and took me home. I promised never to leave school without her again.

While in the village, my grandmother liked me because I was obedient and hardworking. I would help her grind millet to make flour, using a grinding stone. There was a bigger stone and a smaller one. She would put millet grain on the bigger one for her and the smaller one for me. Then I would sing, moving the smaller one to and fro, I would grind the millet flour. I also helped her with fetching water and collecting firewood- these activities were very essential at that time. It was an embarrassment for a girl growing up in a village setting not to know these things.

My grandmother would then make the bread out of the millet flour, while I watched and learned. On three cooking stones, she would light the firewood and put a saucepan filled with water on the stones. She would wait patiently until it boiled. In bits, she would pour in the millet flour, stirring it slowly and cautiously with a mingling stick, making sure the fire was hot enough. When the bread was ready, she would put it in a calabash, turning it around several times to make a round, good-looking shape and then serve it on a plate.

That is how millet bread is made and how I learnt to mingle millet bread.

One day, my grandmother had gone to take cattle to the grazing ground because my grandfather was not around. She instructed us to add more firewood when the ones she had left in the fire got consumed, to make sure that the food that was cooking would be ready by the time she returned. We did so but she took long in the grazing ground and by 3pm we were terribly hungry. So I decided to mingle bread out of the flour that she had kept as I was the eldest girl present. But I did not know how to make it well, and it had to be thrown out when she got back.

Fetching firewood and water were things I helped my grandmother do since she was old and couldn't move long distances. Helping her in these ways gave both of us joy as I was performing my obligation as a child in the village setting. I liked her very much. She used to keep foods like Shea nut oil (*moo yao*) and white ants paste (*ngwen*), which are delicacies that were treasured locally and I felt honored whenever I was served them. In the village I also enjoyed milk from the cows that were from my grandparents' kraal. This was before one pastoral tribe, the Karamojong, raided us and took away cattle. It was a massive raid that affected three tribes that were neighboring them.

I experienced this when my mum took us back to the village in the late 1980s to live with her mother because of war. She thought we were safer in the village, and I studied there for two more years. During this period, I enjoyed my stay in the village so much as life seemed so enjoyable both at home and school.

At school, all the teachers liked me because I could speak English better than any of my peers. The teachers would chat with me in English. I can remember how pupils would gather around me, amazed that I could speak English at such an early age as this was not a common thing in village schools. This was because I learnt English as my first language and studied in a nursery school that taught in English.

I began to learn about the war in northern Uganda in 1986 when President Museveni was taking over the government. I was still young, but I heard what people around me were saying about it. On several occasions I even heard gunshots during clashes between the then government soldiers and the incoming government. But before that, I got to know about violence when the Karamojong (pastoralists) from the northeastern part of Uganda raided all the neighboring tribes of Acholi, Lango and Teso. Several times when I was still living with my grandmother, we had to run and hide in the bush, fearing for our lives when pastoralists raided cattle during the chaos of the war.

On one particular occasion, the pastoralists reached our village at 7am when I had just woken up. My grandmother was grinding, and one of my cousins was still sleeping. We heard gunshots in the distance, and my uncle told us to go hiding as the Karamojong raiders (*olok*) were not far. My grandmother hesitated and was almost caught. Four of us ran with my uncle and survived narrowly after transferring from one hiding place to another under my uncle's order. A bird came and started singing over our heads as we were hiding, and my uncle said that was a bad sign and that we should change positions. After doing so, we heard the raiders talking at the very spot we had just left and we thanked God for saving us.

My cousin, who was sleeping, ran into the bush naked to hide because she had no time to grab anything to cover. Luckily enough she was still young. We stayed in the bush hiding for about eight hours and we could hear the activities of the pastoralists. They were breaking doors, pounding, in order to convince those hiding to come back home so that they could torture them or make them lead them to places where cattle were. This activity caused a lot of suffering among the Langi, Acholi, and the Teso tribes that were neighboring the Karamojong tribe. They grabbed cattle, looted property, raped women and physically tortured whoever they came across. This was the beginning of my suffering. All the cattle that belonged to my grandparents were looted so we had no source of milk any more, and the above three tribes became economically poor because of this rustling.

The war did not end there. When my family moved to live in Gulu where my parents were working in the early 1990s, there was a resistance movement by the Uganda National Liberation Army (UNLA), locally known as *cilil*. In Acholi this means 'go and report'. The good thing then was that they did not attack civilians but only targeted the government soldiers. However, civilians would accidentally be killed during crossfire. As time went on, this rebel group became hostile to even civilians and started killing, looting and abducting people to assist them. Then came Alice Lakwena and finally the Lord's Resistance Army (LRA). I got to know about these groups as I was growing up and heard of their deadly activities, terrorising villages and trading centres, staging ambushes on highways, and even abducting students from institutions. But it was not until I was abducted that I personally felt the impact of the political unrest taking place in northern Uganda in particular.

After my primary leaving exams I went for an interview at St. Mary's College Aboke together with eight other friends of mine. Only two of us were admitted. My parents decided to send me to St. Mary's College Aboke out of the many schools there are in Uganda, because it was then the best secondary school for girls, with high quality education. I remember my mum telling me about St. Mary's when I was just in Primary Four, she said it was a good school for girls, and she wanted me to go to that school if I passed my primary leaving exams. I was excited before ever reaching the school to study there.

It was the best in the sense that both informal and formal education was taught. Informally, we were taught how to live socially and survive in both rural and urban settings. We would dig in the school *shamba* (a field used for growing crops) and learn to keep ourselves and our surroundings clean. All this was taking place alongside the formal education so it was an all-round education.

I also received informal education from my grandmother and my mum. From my mum, I learnt how to cook several dishes, both traditional and other foods, which later helped me when I was in captivity. In addition to household chores, I learnt how to live with people of different characters without being taken up by what they do. I also learnt to be a hardworking person. Informal education is important because it is the basis of formal education. Without it, I believe one is considered irresponsible, undisciplined or even lazy in an

African setting. Also without it one can face hardships when they grow up and this is so for both young men and women. No matter how much our culture is changing I still feel it is important.

Informal education became helpful in the bush because I applied it to help me avoid trouble. For example, my mum taught me to respect elders and avoid unnecessary movements like visiting friends aimlessly. This saved my life in December 1997.

I had a friend who was our student leader back in school but while in the bush, she befriended a man in the hope of getting freedom from the LRA. Their friendship was misinterpreted by the LRA as intimate. This was a deadly offence against their Standing Orders (the rules of the LRA), and so she was beaten to death. I survived because I declined her invitation for a visit. If I had visited her, I would have also been killed with her as they would have believed that she shared her secrets with me about her intention of escape and that we were planning this together. If that had been the case, both of us would have been killed. By sticking to what my mum taught me, I survived that fateful incident. Although I was not happy to see my friend die, there was no way I could save her life.

Back to my life before abduction, it was not all that easy for me to get used to the life in my new school in my village as there was a big gender difference where boys looked at girls as inferior. In my former school girls and boys were treated equally and were calm and disciplined, while kids in my new school were naughty and practiced gender discrimination. The first day of school, I knocked at the door of my primary six class and the teacher allowed me in. As I entered, I saw very many seats unoccupied yet many girls were seated on the floor, and the few boys were seated at the desks. I paused for a while and then made my decision to sit at one of the desks. I saw reactions from the pupils that surprised me. I later learned that I had sat at the desk that was only meant for bright pupils, which in this case were the boys. The girls were considered dull and so were left to sit on the dusty floor, unlike in my former school where everyone would sit at their desk. There was also segregation between boys and girls in terms of performance during that time. Girls were considered dull and the boys were looked at as clever people.

As I was growing up in Uganda, girls and women were not treated in the same way as boys and men were. The latter were taken to be the superior gender. And again, when a child was born between two people who were not married and the child happened to grow up in the maternal family, that child was not respected like the one who grew up with both parents who were married. He or she was referred to as an illegitimate child. So, I got to know about both of the above as I was growing up and heard nasty comments from people regarding illegitimate children. I did not like the idea of a child growing up without parental love and security, so I asked why this was so. The child is innocent. More so, why should the male gender be treated as superior to the female gender yet there are things that females are better at than males, only that they are suppressed by the male gender? So I took a step in school and saw that when it came to academics, even girls were capable of it just like boys, so why the difference?

The other thing that made me think that way is that I saw how painful it was for a woman to be dependent on a man economically, especially in Africa. Most men who have money tend to mistreat their women who do not have any means of getting money to survive on their own, and I concluded basing on the dangers that I witnessed that I would work very hard to avoid such incidences in my life.

Even in the community, there was segregation. People believed that only boys could study, get a job and help their parents later. The girls were taken for granted because they were regarded as people who wouldn't even complete their education but instead get married, therefore spending a lot of effort on their education was a waste of resources. A classmate of mine, a boy with whom I was competing, once made this comment to me. He discouraged me by saying that even if I performed better than him, he was 100% sure that I would drop out of school to marry so he wasn't scared of me.

The girls were scared of the boys and had no voice in class. I wasn't scared of anyone who threatened me so long as I was in the right. I did not mind whatever they said in segregating the girls, for I knew they too were capable of performing well just like the boys, and I even competed with them. In fact, one boy competed with me until senior three because I had performed better than him in primary seven. For the first two years he competed silently without my knowledge and only revealed it to me in our third year of ordinary level that he was waiting to see if I would beat him again in senior four. Unfortunately, I was abducted before I sat for my Ordinary Level Certificate.

# 2

# Abducted

*"...twice we left our school compound to seek a safer place to sleep ... when we heard rumours that LRA rebels were close"*

Our school is located in a quiet place with a fence planted all round. It has many trees and flowers that are always well maintained. From a distance, you can't see the hidden natural beauty of the school grounds, until you take your time to discover it. We were forbidden to leave the compound except on Sundays when we went to church. Every time we went for prayers, our headmistress would mention the name of a girl who had been abducted, but this was the only time I would think of the insecurity.

However, around the time of our abduction, we were instructed to leave the school to sleep in a nearby village. It was so unusual that we became very worried. At most, we had been told to gather our belongings once before and head to town, but this time the rumours that the rebels were planning to abduct girls from our school abounded. Still, we were warned by our headmistress not to say anything about the insecurity. Anyone who was caught discussing anything concerning the rebels would be expelled instantly.

On that evening we were told to sleep in the village, we took only our bed sheets and slept on mats in somebody's homestead that had many huts. The following morning we headed for school, feeling safe as we moved past several grass thatched houses to find our way back to school, using a narrow, slippery road that connected St. Mary's College Aboke to the village. Yet as we entered the school gate one-by-one, we were surprised to meet a group of 12 armed men and a woman finding their way out of the school. The sight of the soldiers was so strange to us! We had never seen any gunmen in the school compound. These were a group of Local Defense Unit (LDU) that was brought to guard the school in case the rebels attacked that night. We suspected that the security was not okay as soldiers had never guarded us before.

On reaching the school, we bathed and got organised for the day as it was a holiday, the day Uganda got its independence, the 9th of October. This was a day that was celebrated nationally and according to the normal school program we were to go to church in the morning from 10 a.m. up to midday then take lunch at exactly 1 pm. Then, from 2-6 pm, there was entertainment (dancing). From 6 to 6.30 pm, we would say the rosary. And at 7 pm we were to have supper. Lastly, we were supposed to watch movies up to 10 pm, and then retire to bed. But the program did not flow the way it was supposed to that day. It so happened that as we were saying the rosary, a military helicopter gunship landed in a nearby primary school and this increased our worry about what was going on as it was very strange! We worried even more that rebels were nearby. We started wondering what would happen in the night as the sun was already setting. Students started imagining and discussing very many strange things about the LRA, like an incident that had happened a month earlier, when the LRA had raided a secondary school, Sir Samuel Baker, in a neighboring district of Gulu, and abducted schoolboys.

So, on that fateful night of 9th October 1996, instead of watching movies, our headmistress, Sister Alba, asked us to go to bed early since a heavy rain was about to pour, and the night was windy and dark. As she normally called us children, she said, *"Children go to bed. A big storm is coming and we are going to have an early night."* The electricity failed and it was pitch black outside. We went to bed but were afraid of what would happen in the night as it was extremely dark and we could only see the tall eucalyptus trees and the banana plantation that was behind our dormitories when lightning flashed.

Not sure of our security this time, we slept fitfully. I woke up in the night at around 1 am and felt like easing myself but was afraid because it was extremely dark outside, so I went back to bed as I waited for anyone who felt the same to accompany me out to the pit latrine. As I was waiting for a potential companion, I heard footsteps of a person coming towards the door from behind but nobody ever reached the door. Unfortunately, the footsteps that I heard belonged to the enemy.

After about thirty minutes, I saw a torch being flashed into the dormitory from one side and I knew at once that we were in danger. I had never before seen someone using a torch at that early hour of the morning. My heart started pumping very fast in fear as I found my way under my bed to hide. After flashing for a while, I heard the stranger saying, *"There are no people here."* He could not see anyone as all the girls who were sleeping on the upper beds were hiding under the lower beds. But they must have spotted us from another window and the stranger ordered that the door be opened in a local language (Acholi). After hearing that, we knew they were rebels! From then I started hearing deep male voices from outside the dormitory and others were threatening to burn the dormitory down if we refused to open the door. One spoke in English saying *"Open the door. We will not harm you. We are also students like you."* This turned out to be a student who had been abducted the previous month from Sir Samuel Baker School, the boys' school in Gulu. He spoke in an attempt to convince us to open the door for them but we did not.

On the other hand, from inside, girls were unsettled, quaking and moving up and down in fear. The next step by the rebels to find their way into the dormitory was violent. They started throwing big stones at the glass windows and broke them. The broken glass even injured a few girls. Others used axes to break the wall and remove the window frame so as to get into the dormitory. In minutes, the rebels were in and we were at their mercy, shaking in fear in our nightwear.

The first to enter our dormitory was a huge, dark-skinned man who ordered us in a deep, scary voice to switch on the light and get out of the dormitory. In our night dresses, we moved outside helplessly, shaking both from fear and the cold. They then tied our hands backwards like the police do when handling criminals. As they did this, other rebels were looting our belongings like clothes from the hooks, foodstuffs, and sandals.

In the dark, chilly night, we stood outside our dormitories waiting for them to complete their mission of looting our belongings and waited for our fate. With our hands tied, we were marched in a single line out of the school gate like slaves in the hands of their masters. There was no one to defend us, not even the government soldiers who had guarded the school the previous day were there while we were being abducted.

As I stepped out of the school gate, I watched our school dispensary being looted and a Reverend Deacon from the nearby parish being dragged into our school with his hands tied, while behind him two motor vans were blazing. In horror, I took one step after the other, numb, into the darkness, wondering where our headmistress, the deputy and the gatekeeper were. As the whole school was flooded with rebels, there was no school authority or administrator who showed up to defend us. All this while, I was wondering whether they were hiding while we were being stolen away from school where we hoped to study for a brighter future. On our feet on a wet, muddy path, we kept widening the distance between the school, and ourselves to an unknown destination in the dark.

As it was approaching dawn, I could see some of the rebels guarding us were young boys of about twelve years old, carrying guns that seemed to be heavier than them. They wore dirty, ragged, army uniforms. Some had braided hair while others had unkempt hair with fierce-looking red eyes that communicated only danger. This was so horrible to me and

I kept on thinking of how my fate would be in the hands of these people who appeared so merciless.

Among the rebels, I also recognised two familiar faces of boys whom I had studied with in primary school and were now in their teens. I could not believe my eyes at first, for they had guns already and were actively participating in the rebel activity. When I got the courage to ask one boy who remembered me as well how they got involved, he told me that they had been abducted from school a month earlier and forcefully given the guns to fight. This kept me wondering as I moved and in the process I knocked my toe seriously against a stump that led to a permanent dislocation which lasts till today. The pain I felt cannot be expressed in words. I fell down instantly together with three other friends I was tied to using the same rope. I got up and started limping and carried on with the never-ending journey that led us to a meeting point deep in the bush. This was a cumbersome long walk, running and hiding from danger that took us a whole day. As we rested, we were surprised to see the arrival of our deputy headmistress, a nun, Sister Rachelle, around ten in the morning. On seeing her, our hopes of being freed rose. In fact, we had heard the rebels had abducted girls from our school before, but were released when the nuns insisted they should be released and so we thought that would be the case with us. However, the rebels ignored her and we kept on moving until 1 pm when the rebel commander summoned us to stop and gather together. All the schoolgirls from St. Mary's were ordered to assemble under a tree so that an agreement could be arrived at in regards to our release.

Tired, hungry and helpless, we gathered under the shade of a big tree to listen to what Major Lagira — the short, fat and dark-skinned commander with red eyes and a swollen upper lip — had to say to us. Unfortunately, a helicopter gunship belonging to the Ugandan government circled over us, and we were dispersed under the commander's order as they realised the government soldiers were pursuing us. On hearing gunshots from a short distance, they started harassing us to run ahead as a few of them remained to face the government soldiers. Gathering our last reserves of strength we obeyed their order and moved ahead. We followed their instructions to be careful when moving, most especially with the gunship, as it could easily drop bombs on us if we did not move under cover since we were not wearing camouflage attire. The movement then changed from slow to fast, mixed with running plus hiding under bushes, as instructed by the rebels in an attempt to save our lives. I remember Sister Rachelle was given somebody's black attire to cover her white veil.

It was late in the evening when we reached a homestead surrounded by a banana plantation and that day's journey finally came to a halt. In total, the 139 girls were able to reach here. We assembled again to listen to the final command of Major Lagira.

The other tall, dark-skinned man who had ordered us from our dormitory shortly arrived and we waited impatiently for the final judgment like that of God which always comes when one dies. He (the tall and dark one) started picking on the girls one at a time and asking each one's name, tribe, area of residence and the individual's class. In doing so, we realised there were two groups being created. He went on asking those who had injuries to join the larger group and since I had knocked my right toe, I got up to join that group but the man told me to remain standing while he selected and separated the remaining girls. Wondering which group I would be asked to join, I remained standing, speechless.

Again, when only eight girls were left seated, he ordered them to join the bigger group, and I moved with them but he strongly warned me not to move a step. I got so disturbed and confused, wondering what I might have done to provoke the man's anger. Finally I was in the group with few girls but unfortunately that was the group that was remaining in the bush while the members in the bigger group were to be set free. On hearing that I was among the 30 girls who would remain with the rebels, I was shocked and all sorts of thoughts started running in my mind like 'Why me or only the thirty of us? What next? Will I survive or not? What about my education, don't these rebels know that education is our future?' We then burst into loud cries for Sister Rachelle to plead with the rebels to let us go. All those efforts did not bear fruit, instead, the result was terrible! Major Lagira gave an order to his boys to give us strokes of the cane, and they did exactly as told. We were properly beaten and stepped on with the rough soles of their gumboots that left many of us injured. On seeing this, Sister Rachelle pleaded with Major Lagira to release all of us, but on hearing this plea, he even became more hostile and he threatened to retain the freed 109 girls in addition to the 30. While weeping, she promised never to sit down or rest until all of us were released. On hearing this, we got some courage and hope since we knew her as a determined person, who always meant what she said. Since it was getting dark, we painfully watched her leave with the 109 girls, as we remained in total darkness with strangers. From that moment, I lost even the little hope I had for my future.

## Left behind

Later in the night, we were summoned and briefed by Major Lagira on the do's and don'ts in the LRA. We were separated into groups of six and distributed to the five battalions that were in that brigade that very night for easy supervision. I remained in a section called Operation Room that was commanded by Captain Oyet, the one who participated in selecting us. I loathed this man because he contributed a lot to my remaining behind with the rebels.

That evening, we were given boiled goat meat and *posho* (food made from ground maize flour) to eat after an initiation called *wir* (cleansing/initiation). Our palms, foreheads, chests, backs and legs were smeared while making a sign of the cross using special oil made from locally-made shea nut butter (*moo yaa/yao*). As explained to us, it was to show that from then on, we belonged to the LRA. In my heart, however, I was quietly saying, "*No matter what you do, I know I will not belong here forever.*" This initiation was done before eating. Before then we were not supposed to come into contact (like greeting, eating or accessing anything that they used) with the members called 'the originals' as we were considered unclean.

Having moved the whole day without eating or drinking, I was happy and washed my hands to eat with full appetite but when I tasted the food, I was discouraged as it tasted different from the goat meat I always ate at home. With the soup smelling of raw meat, I decided to sleep hungry. We were then packed into a very small hut together with some of the new captives. In normal circumstances, such a hut would accommodate only five people but over twenty people were forced inside irrespective of their gender and age, all of them newly abducted. I will live to remember that horrible night where I sat awake the whole night, sweating, squeezed and extremely hot due to the congestion, with the worst picture of what would happen to me the following morning.

At dawn, I imagined how beautiful and bright the sun would emerge from the east as it brought new hope for the day. But there I was on a bright morning with a clear blue sky in the hands of the cruel rebels with whom my own life was at risk. Relieved from the horrible condition in the small hut, I got out once again into the fresh morning breeze that could not even be dreamt of in the night. Within my heart I kept pondering my fate in the new environment. I asked for water to clean my face and sat under a shade waiting for what would happen next. It was not long until I heard Captain Oyet whistle. This was a signal used to alert everyone that it was time to leave or get on the move either to change position or when they realised their enemies were close.

On seeing me barefoot, one girl who had already been with the LRA for two years offered me a pair of new sandals, and there the long journey to an unknown destination started again. The sandals relieved me of the pain I was feeling in my soles as we marched in a single line, heading North. After walking for about two miles, I saw a helicopter but I was not bothered as I had not known it as a dangerous machine. The next thing I saw were the rebels taking cover under big trees and cautioning us who were new in the movement to hide for safety. At the same time, able men with bare chests were running back to where we came from at a terrific speed with their guns ready for action. This created a lot of fear in me and my heart pumped so hard that even my guard, who was already pointing a gun at me, could hear.

In no time, I heard gunshots from both machine guns and bombs just a few meters away from where we were hiding. This increased my fear even more, as it was my first time to hear gunshots in a battle field. So scared of the sound, I was unsettled in my position and wanted to run away but I couldn't as I was under guard. I could hear soldiers in the frontline shouting in between gunshots running towards us, but the rebels defeated the government soldiers and they did not reach us. Rather, their shouting kept on reducing. Meanwhile, the helicopter gunship with its scary sound in the air was seriously bombing all around us. The state of fear I was in cannot be expressed in words, but my soul had left my body for a while, and I was cold, speechless and only waiting for my last breath.

What almost made me go crazy was the sight of wounded LRA fighters who were bleeding due to injuries they had sustained from the frontline. It was as if I was feeling the pain myself though I was not injured. Instantly, I developed a terrible headache and pain in my entire joints as I saw one wounded LRA commander being carried on a temporary stretcher. He had been shot on the upper arm and blood was oozing from his wound as he cried aloud in pain for help, saying in anger, *"If you people cannot help me stop the bleeding then leave me to die."* He was lamenting and blaming us, the schoolgirls, for having caused his pain. I think if he had gotten hold of a gun, he would have not spared any of us as he even kicked one girl right on the head from the stretcher where he was being carried by four other newly abducted men.

After the guns went silent, we were ordered to get on the move while at the same time hiding from the helicopter gunship that was still bombing randomly at the rebels. From 11 am we got on our toes following paths among villages, crossing rivers, climbing hills, heading northwards in a single line. We were all marching and exhausted but the journey was unending. In addition to the hectic, long journey, what nagged me most was having to give way for those who were carrying wounded soldiers. They would time and again ask those in the line to give way for them to pass but then they would get tired so fast and stop to rest. After, they would again ask us to give way, which became very tiresome. Because of the heavy weight of the casualty being carried on the improvised stretcher, wounds developed on the shoulders of the men carrying them. I pitied them because of the pain on their shoulders and the task of carrying the wounded. I strongly believe in God so I kept on praying and asking Him to help me out of the situation.

I was relieved when the long chain of people came to a halt in the evening. Exhausted, with my ankles aching, I sat down and only asked for water to drink to quench my thirst. Since there was nothing much I could do, I only looked for a knife for cutting grass, which I spread down as my bed for that night. Then together with my two other friends, we slept sharing the same piece of bedsheet we were given. We slept facing the same direction with our backs turned to one another such that when one person wished to turn, then all three of us would turn at the same time so as to fit in the small bed and dustcoat that we were given for a bedsheet. That ended my third day in the bush.

Over the next two weeks, the order of the day was waking up early in the morning and moving around from village to village searching for food, dodging the government soldiers for a few hours and then camping in a position to cook and eat. Whenever the rebels and the government soldiers met, they would engage in a serious exchange of fire. While moving, all sorts of foodstuff like groundnuts and *sim-sim* (sesame seeds) would be looted from villages, as well as cows, goats, chicken, cassava and potatoes. These were loaded on the newly abducted persons. On reaching a suitable place where there was an adequate water supply and good security, allocation of positions (where each person should spend the night) was done by Captain Oyet, who was an operation commander under the command of Major Lagira. Major Lagira would rest at the center of the temporary camp called a position, surrounded by other commanders with lower ranks. On reaching the position, activities like fetching water, washing clothes, bathing, cooking, and nursing wounds of the injured were done. The same position could be held for up to two days if the security was good and if there weren't any planned missions ahead.

For two solid months, that was the life I lived with the rebels while in Uganda, until one day I asked Captain Oyet why we were being kept in the bush yet there wasn't anything productive we were doing. I went on to ask him to let us go as they were wasting our time for studies. His answer to me was so surprising; he said we had been captured for a reason that was prophesied by Joseph Kony, the LRA leader. Kony had ordered for our abductions from St. Mary's College Aboke, as he was instructed by his spirits that he should go to our school and select only thirty girls who would make the world know about the existence of the Lord's Resistance Movement and their operation in the northern part of Uganda. That is how I got to know that our presence there was a fulfillment of what was foresaid by the spirits.

### Physical torture

One morning as we were leaving a position, Major Lagira confronted a group of schoolgirls and asked, "*Why is the whole world concerned about the Aboke abductions including the Pope? Doesn't the Pope know that the LRA is fighting for the ten commandments of God? Since the Pope made a nasty comment about LRA by asking the rebels to release all the school girls captured from Aboke, you are to be punished and you should forget about your release and studies from this day forward and put into your minds that you are soldiers and no longer students.*" On hearing this, I could not believe my ears. We started discussing the matter amongst us and doubted our freedom. The case did not end only in questions but it proceeded into our serious beatings when we reached the next position. Major Lagira summoned all of us and ordered his escorts to bring canes for beating us. We were all panicking and pleading with him to pardon us but all our pleas were in vain as energetic boys advanced towards us with huge canes in their hands and ordered us to lie facing down. Shivering in fear, we waited to receive the painful strokes of the cane.

Having received fifteen strokes, I could hardly sit on my backside as this was the part of my body that was affected. Even mere walking would cause me pain, and on touching it, I could feel marks that were lining my buttocks horizontally, the way the cane landed. It took weeks for my wounds to heal and I became so bitter with Major Lagira for his cruelty that always aimed at torturing people without genuine reasons, most especially the newly abducted whom they used to refer to as *okurut* (recruits).

Physical torture did not end there but it continued even as we kept on moving around villages. One day in particular as we were moving in a single line one after the other, one boy made an attempt to escape but he was caught in the act red-handed. I had not known about this until I heard Major Lagira complain about the recruits as we were moving. He said that since most recruits were escaping he was going to show them fire that day. In my heart I was imagining how hot it would be in terms of torture. On reaching the position, all recruits were summoned under Lagira's order.

Only this announcement was enough to make me break down in tears as I waited for my fate in the next few minutes. The boy who was caught trying to escape was a younger brother to one of the boys who had stayed with the rebels for a year already. I felt so sad to hear Lagira call the boy to come and say goodbye to his younger brother who was caught escaping. Lagira ordered the elder one to say, "*My brother, you came and found me here alive but decided to run away. Now that you are going to die, all because of your stupidity, go well.*" I felt so sad and tears rolled down my cheeks in pity for the little innocent boy who was seeking nothing but freedom from the rebels.

All recruits who had been with the rebels for less than two months in the bush were told to lie down flat, to be initiated into the army. They inflicted pain on us so that we would never think of escaping the LRA. We all lay down in a very large courtyard, with our heads facing down in the hot sand. Seated on a chair, Lagira gave orders, "*Hey boys! You can now walk, jump, run or do whatever pleases you on these people.*" So, soldiers wearing gumboots with rough soles stepped and jumped on our backs. They tortured us. I could hear so many people groaning in pain under Lagira's command. For us who were lying down, we were not to lift our heads to see who was stepping on whom. So I kept my head down but felt a very heavy weight right on my back, which nearly prevented me from breathing as my chest bone was pressed so hard on the ground. That was just the first order.

The second order was for us to be caned and two energetic LRA soldiers were to handle one recruit. Using a method called *brigade* the soldiers beat us at the same time until they were stopped. This is one of the most severe ways of instilling the spirit of being a soldier that I experienced, for one could be beaten for as long as fifteen minutes non-stop. Following the initiation, it was like we were in a children's ward, in a hospital, where each one of us was expressing aloud the pain they felt by either wailing, making an alarm, moaning or groaning. Major Lagira only stopped the beating exercise after he was satisfied the degree of pain we were feeling was great enough. The pain I felt was unbelievable. I thought I was dreaming but it was real. My whole body was aching in pain. My head, back, buttocks, and legs were all swollen. To my surprise, soldiers were amused that those of us who had been beaten were limping, weak and others had fainted. I wondered how inhumane the LRA soldiers were. They claimed to be fighting for the ten commandments of God and yet they were not practicing what they preached. The rebels' happiest moments were seeing someone in pain.

As if the first two punishments were not enough, Major Lagira called for all the girls abducted from Aboke to kill someone. At this point, there were 15 of us; the other 15 were in another battalion. This exercise was to make us part of the rebels, so that we would not think of escaping anymore. So the young boy who was caught escaping was led into the bush where he was to be murdered with both of his hands tied and his eyes covered with a piece of cloth. Under tight security, we moved in a single line into a nearby bush and came to a halt under a huge tree where he was told to lie facing down. We were told to beat his head in turns with big, heavy sticks. We were surrounded by gun men with bayonets threatening to kill whoever was scared to hit the boy right on his head.

One of my friends who had turned her face away from the boy in fear after one soldier had demonstrated how to kill was singled out to be the first to hit the boy. She stretched her hands high in fear and hit the boy right on his head with all her might and he died instantly. What she did relieved all of us from the fear we had of being forced to hit and kill which is a crime against God for those who believe. We were all sad that the boy was killed innocently, but relieved that our friend had finished the hard task. Since we missed the killing 'game', we were ordered to step on the dead boy's head.

Scared and already sick of the horrible sight of the poor boy's smashed head, I didn't want to step on him, so when it came to my turn to step on the boy, I stepped on his legs instead of his head and this became an offence that I had to account for. One tall, thin and dark young officer confronted me and told me to bend and turn the nape of my neck to him. I got so scared and thought I would breathe my last. On bending, he gave me just one stroke of the cane on the nape and that was enough to make me feel dizzy and see stars. I will never forget the pain that I felt on being beaten. Helpless, scared and with my whole body aching from that day's torture, I carried myself slowly back to the position where I recovered from the dizziness but psychologically and physically, I was badly tormented.

In just less than two months, I had seen more than enough to make me predict how uncertain life would be in the LRA, judging from the many horrific things ranging from those that affected me directly to those that I saw with my naked eyes happening to people in villages we passed. I saw the legs of two people being cut off by the rebels. The first incident was in a place called Awac in Gulu district. It was in the evening when we approached the village and I heard those who were conversant with directions saying we were in Awac. We came across a man riding a bicycle. He was stopped instantly and blamed for having broken one of the rules that were set by the LRA in which riding a bicycle was prohibited. They had written a note earlier on warning civilians not to ride bicycles. This was to prevent civilians from reporting their whereabouts to government soldiers. The LRA strongly believed that they endured constant attacks from government soldiers because of civilians passing on information to them. So they wanted to frighten villagers from reporting to the army by using violence. When the man was found riding, he was first asked whether he was aware that the LRA is against riding. This was late in the evening, and the sun was almost setting. His answer was positive. He was then told that his leg would be cut for the crime he had committed. Shocked, surprised and pleading for pardon, the man could not believe his ears but patiently waited for his fate. Major Lagira asked for an axe, which was used by his escort to chop off the man's leg. It was put on his bike and practically cut between the shin and the ankle like a piece of wood, blood started oozing out very fast. I looked at the man with a lot of pity as part of his leg lay in a pool of blood, never to be used again.

In less than two days, the same incident occurred, but this time in another village called Pabbo. We came across a man together with his mother and younger brother by the roadside. On seeing us, the man picked his bicycle and rode very fast for safety after realising that those were the rebels. The next thing the rebels did was blame the woman for pre-informing her son to ride away, either way he was brought back. The scenario was horrifying. The woman was told to bite her son's leg until it bled for having ridden a bicycle. With her missing front teeth, she started struggling to bite her son's leg, but it was all in vain. Later an axe was used to cut off the man's leg. I felt so bad and said to myself, *"Why do these people (rebels) think of only punishments and torture that inflict pain on people like this?"*

After moving with the LRA for nearly two months with no hope of escaping or being released, I started planning to escape with Evelyn, who was my classmate. Our plan was to run away in our own directions in case of any attack because we could not make it as a group with my other schoolmates, as our security was so tight. Each of the thirty of us had a guard who was to be killed if anyone of us escaped. So they all did their best to stop us from escaping. After discussing with Evelyn, she moved ahead to catch up with her guard who would punish her if she (the guard) reached the position before Evelyn.

With only eight people between me and her, I heard very many gunshots ahead of us suddenly, and I could see those who were in front retreating. Unknowingly, we had entered an ambush that had been laid by the side of one of the main roads. In response, I turned to the right and ran as fast as my legs could carry me as numerous bullets flew at us like rain falling from the heavens. I felt like the bullets were aiming at wherever I was stepping because I could hear them falling as I was running for my dear life. I found myself leading in the run and paving my way in my own direction without a guard.

I thought at once that it was my time to be free but I was being followed. To my surprise, I was ordered to stop after being recognised by my school sweater and so that attempt failed. We treked back to cross the main road at the same spot where we had earlier on been ambushed and crossed at a terrible speed for fear of another attack. On crossing to the other side of the road, I saw that most of those who had crossed before us were wounded by the bullets from the government army, and I got so worried about the safety of my friends, the other schoolgirls. They meant a lot to me. There was an attachment that had grown amongst us since our abduction. We were like sisters and whatever happened to one was a concern to all. It was not until later in the evening that I got the message that Evelyn had succeeded in escaping, just the way we had planned. I wished I had followed her and escaped, but it was impossible and too late.

## Hope for release

After this incident, Joseph Kony decided that we should all be taken to Sudan straight away to stop us from escaping. He sent his immediate deputy, George Omona (also known as Field Commander) to Uganda from Sudan to release us. On hearing the news we were happy and hopeful, I started imagining being home and how it would be like after being snatched away from school. I also imagined how much water I would use for bathing and the kind of deworming tablets I would take after having drunk dirty water several times, but life turned out to be completely different from what I was thinking. Just reaching where Joseph Kony's second-in-command was became a tug of war as it took us two days to reach there after moving for long distances without food or water. I got very tired, sick and weak, as I developed a very serious headache after eating a kind of root tuber (cassava that was meant only for making local brew) due to lack of food. Moreover, we were being pursued by the government troops. We had to cross from one district to another for safety. I remember on the day before reaching, I was feeling terribly hungry after the day's journey and came across a banana plantation. I saw energetic boys and girls coming out of the plantation with ripe bananas, and I also rushed there to get some for myself but there was nothing left. Feeling very disappointed, I moved sluggishly back to my position but fortunately met a girl who was kind enough to give me just a banana after I asked. On eating the banana, I gained a lot of strength and felt so happy as it filled my empty stomach and relieved my hunger. From then on I believed that any little thing given wholeheartedly means a lot to someone getting it, more than a treasure given without love. What I will not forget is crossing the Aswa River. I had not seen such a mass of water flowing at that speed in my life because there isn't any big water body in my home area. When we were told that we would cross the river, my stomach churned in fear and I wondered how I would cross without any knowledge of swimming. To make matters worse, the strong water current carried the first seven people away. Seeing them struggling and crying for help, with no one willing to help scared me, they disappeared in the fast flowing water never to be heard of again.

The river was wide, and it was flowing very fast with hard rocks in its bed. Without a boat, I could not picture how we were going to cross. Moreover, we were being pursued by the government troops. Fortunately, I saw the best swimmers crossing the river with a long, thick rope that was tied on both sides of the river. We were to use this to cross. I could not believe it was possible to cross a wide, fast flowing river using just a rope until I saw it. For the first twenty people, I observed the skills they used to overcome the strong current and asking from the experienced ones the process of crossing safely. I learnt that for one to reach safely, he or she was to hold on tight to the rope and move his or her hands while being mindful of the current without any heavy luggage on their backs, until they reached the other side of the river. This was so scary because it was as though they were flying on water due to the strong current, with only their hands holding tightly onto the rope and their heads lifted up to prevent them from taking in water. I prayed quietly in my heart, *"God, help me and save my life today."* So when my turn came, I stepped into the water together with six other people and held tightly onto the rope. We moved slowly until I reached a point where the current was so strong. It was between life and death as the people were shouting from either side that if I left the rope that would be the end of me. So I managed to reach the other side of the river safely following the instructions given and what I did next was to thank my God who gave me the strength.

The next thing was climbing up the hill as the river is in a valley. It was late in the evening when I reached the position. Tired, hungry and wet, I sat down to check in the small luggage that I was carrying for some groundnuts to eat, but did not get any. I learned it was taken by an original so I got the courage to confront her and tell her that what she did was wrong, that she should also treat us like human beings. I had observed earlier on that the originals consumed all the food, leaving out the new recruits. They would send us to do work as they ate all the food and left us hungry. At times they would roast for themselves cassava and groundnuts and exclude us, the recruits, hence leaving us to starve. I told her that everyone needed to eat, including the recruits. What she was doing was wrong, she should have thought about other people as she wasn't the only one to feeling hungry.

After that, we also copied their survival strategies to live among them. I remember one day I participated in struggling to grab unshelled groundnuts from somebody's granary and even uprooted cassava from people's gardens in order to survive and stock for future use as we moved on with life waiting for when we will get our freedom. So in the LRA, it was always survival of the fittest when it came to food.

With so much excitement about our release, I woke up very early the following morning in order to clean my face and brush my teeth using a stick so I could prepare myself in time to meet George Omona, the one sent by Joseph Kony to release us. Dressed in my usual long, brown skirt and the same school sweater I had been wearing all this time, I joined the other schoolgirls all in their school sweaters to meet the Field Commander, as he was commonly called. We were assembled like bottles of soda to be presented to the boss. No sooner had we reached than the shelling began. This was a random attack by the enemy using bombs like RPGs (rocket propeller guns) and mortar from a distance to disorganise us. It was like we were being watched from the other side of the river as the shooter aimed exactly where we were. That attack ended our face-to-face meeting with the field commander and never did we hear anything else to do with our release. Later we got sad news that we were not set free because one LRA commander acted as an obstacle to our freedom. He had fallen deeply in love with one of us to the point that letting us go meant losing his sweetheart. So when he was asked to give his opinion regarding our release, he simply said, *"These girls are already used to the lifestyle in the bush, so there is no need of releasing them."* And that was enough to block the way to our freedom. That was how we ended up staying in the LRA for years and five others ended up losing their lives.

This made us angry to the point that we really criticised our friend's behavior and we blamed her for all the sufferings that we encountered later on our way to Sudan, plus all that we encountered in our stay there. Worst of all, it was raining in the night. With no shelter in my position, I would sleep on dry grass with all my clothes wet. It would be so cold the only heat I felt came from my body. I blamed her for the boil that started in a simple way but turned into a very painful wound on my right leg. This wound tormented me to the point that I grew thin due to pain that was increased by the sharp blades of grass that brushed it while I was moving. The pain I felt cannot be explained in words, but I felt it deep in my soul.

Every day we would wake up, move, run and hide for the sake of our lives. Little did we know that one of our friends brought up an issue that would have cost us our lives. We were surprised one morning when we were called urgently to Major Lagira's position and asked threatening questions that most of us had no clue about. At the same time he ordered his bodyguards to cut sticks for caning us. On seeing sticks being cut, we got so scared that he was going to beat us seriously without any reason as usual. We were to openly confess whether any of us were being sexually harassed by any male so far since our abduction. Each one of us kept on looking at the other's face in surprise and at the same time enquiring whether any of us had ever been sexually abused.

We had one girl who did not speak the local language, and we translated to her what was being said. It was then that she told us that one commander, a second lieutenant by the name of Obwoya, convinced her that all the other schoolgirls in other positions had also been given out as wives to the respective commanders who were taking care of them, which wasn't the case, and this made her accept to engage in a sexual act with the man. This, as we got to know, was a serious offence against the LRA Standing Orders and the penalty was death straight away. It was unfortunate that I had just been transferred to that commander's battalion straight away I got to know that I was not in safe hands.

One thing that I admired about the LRA was their strictness when it came to moral behavior in regard to sexual acts. It was against their Standing Orders to abduct a female and abuse her sexually. The penalty was instant death. On realising that the girl who was abused did not know how to express herself in the local language, she was pardoned but otherwise a couple caught violating this order was to be shot by the firing squad. After dispersing us, I went back to my position where Obwoya was and he asked me why we had been called. When I explained to him, his mood changed and I saw fear in him for he realised he was not safe. Major Lagira called him soon after, and that was the last time I saw him that day. He was given two hundred strokes of the cane and was held in custody for the night, as he waited for the last order from the boss, Joseph Kony.

The following morning at around 10 am, everyone in the group under the command of Major Lagira was summoned to listen to what Obwoya had done and witness his punishment as well. His punishment was to serve as a warning to the rest of us. Standing in a very large courtyard, we stood quietly as Lagira pronounced Obwoya's punishment as communicated from Sudan by the LRA leader. Obwoya was then brought in bare-chested with his hands tied and condemned before everyone for his act. A few boys later led him to a nearby bush where they killed him.

# 3

# Journey to Sudan

*"...I had in my mind...that we were going to be sold as slaves to the Arabs."*

Sudan is a country neighboring Uganda to the north. It was where the LRA rebel base was located, and where the training of recruits took place. According to what I was told by one of the girls who had stayed with the rebels for five years, life in Sudan was extremely hard and harsh. Most of the LRA soldiers dodged going back to Sudan whenever they realised that the movement was northwards towards the south of Sudan which they used to call 'Kampala' or 'city'.

She told me of how the recruits would die of starvation or diseases like cholera, the long, tiresome journey to reach the place, and worst of all the risks involved in the process of moving. I imagined Sudan to be a dangerous place to live in. When I inquired how long it would take to reach Sudan, I was told that it takes about a week. Then I told one of my friends with whom I was in the same position *"Even if the security is tight, we can still escape and come back to Uganda after moving into Sudan."*

Major Lagira ordered everyone to carry enough food, as we would soon enter a no-food zone. The security on the recruits was tightening and the direction of movement was northwards but I could tell from my little knowledge in geography that we were heading to Sudan. The only thing that I had in my mind was that we were going to be sold as slaves to the Arabs because of the West African history that I studied at school, where I learnt that Arabs are slave traders. So with deep pain, I imagined how brutally slaves were treated and pictured myself in that situation. And even when I was still at home I would hear people around me say that Joseph Kony abducts young boys and girls, takes them to Sudan and exchanges them for war weapons. To worsen the situation, he had ordered his commanders to handle us schoolgirls with extra care so that we would arrive in good condition. I thought, *"Maybe he wants us in good condition so that we cost a little bit more than the rest."*

On the first day, we were heading to cross one of the main roads at Palabek in the extreme north of Uganda at night. It was not so easy to cross because government soldiers in most cases would be waiting to ambush any LRA convoy that was crossing the road. In case they bumped into each other, serious exchanges of fire took place and the end result was massive loss of life on both sides or injuries were sustained. This made crossing main roads a very big risk for it was a matter of life and death. When crossing, about fifteen stand-by soldiers were sent to check on the safety of the road before the whole group crossed. In case there were no soldiers, then the LRA convoy followed and crossed the road running.

## Attempt to escape

By then my dear friend Lisa and I had planned to escape when crossing the road. Two days before that, one commander, Labongo, called both of us and said that somebody from Sudan had dreamt that we were planning to escape. He warned us that if we had that plan in mind then we should make sure that both of us escaped at once because if one of us remained, she would have to die in place of the other who had gone. So we planned to escape together.

On a hot sunny day at around 3 pm, we set off in a single line to cross the main road under tight security after standby. One after the other, with loads containing foodstuff and heavy guns that were mostly carried by recruits, we moved and whenever we got tired, we rested for a short period and proceeded. It was not until later in the evening that I realised that my friend was nowhere to be seen, because we all had different female bodyguards I asked those who knew her where she was but they told me that she was far behind. This message discouraged me from our initial plan of escape but I did not give up. I just bumped into two security guards who were telling people to run as fast as they could because the main road was only a few miles from their position. On seeing them, I increased my speed to avoid being beaten as they did to those who were moving slowly. It was already dark when I crossed the main road, panting and sweating all over after running for a long distance.

I could not carry out my escape plan because some of the LRA soldiers were heavily guarding the road. Since it was dark, I thought of another plan to get myself out of the bush (from the rebels). The new plan was to branch from the line and hide until everyone had gone and then go back to the main road and follow it to the nearest town, Kitgum, and then proceed to my hometown.

My new plan seemed so smart to me but again I was acting out of ignorance. Little did I know that whenever the LRA moved, there were always five dangerous guards who moved far behind the main group and their main work was to safeguard the convoy as they moved and to kill whoever they got in their way since they were supposed to be the last people. The killing was done regardless of any condition like sickness or even those who could not walk anymore because of blisters on their feet. They would not even spare those whose luggage was too heavy for them to continue any more.

With my two saucepans wrapped in a piece of cloth on my back, I glanced back and saw no one coming from the trail, and from in front too so I made sure that there was quite a distance between the person I was following and me to avoid being noticed. I stepped into the nearby bush and hid myself. I had hidden for only 15 minutes when I remembered that Lisa and I had made an agreement not to leave each other. I thought of the consequences of my escape to her since we had been forewarned and I emerged from my hiding place. Unfortunately, I bumped into one cruel soldier who shouted at me in trying to inquire who was guarding me as no schoolgirl was allowed to be alone. He recognised me because of my school sweater.

I was so scared since he was holding an axe, I ran ahead to join four other people who were passing so he got confused and could not trace me easily in the dark. I lost track after two aborted attempts to escape because I kept thinking of my fate if my friend Lisa escaped, or Lisa's fate if I escaped. This was because we moved in a place with very thick vegetation and extremely dark. In order to move well, one had to hold on to another's shirt or dress to avoid missing the person in front as we could not see anything. I tried to trace the trail but failed. From behind, people were stranded and confused about where to go. One man in particular came forward in search of the one who had caused the breakage in the line but I turned back and hid among the others. He quarreled and cursed the person but I kept quiet as he did not recognise me.

The trail was later discovered and we proceeded with the journey to the position, where I got the bad news that 'Lisa' had not yet reached the position. This disorganised me even more because I imagined myself being killed or seriously beaten because she had escaped and I decided on two things: to either go back and then get caught  red-handed escaping or wait for some time then take another course of action. I decided to wait for her arrival first. For over two hours I was unsettled, moving up and down regretting why I had come out of my hiding place and at the same time praying that at least Lisa would show up to save both of us. I could not go away not knowing if she had escaped because she would have been killed.

To my relief, I saw her coming and I joyously ran to meet her. When she saw me, she said, *"All I was thinking of was whether I will still get you around or only come to die after you have left, but thank God you are around. Let's try our luck again."* We went together to the position. The bond that had developed among us since our abduction was too strong to be broken. We felt like we were from one family such that one person's problem was a concern to all. That is why I could not leave Lisa to die.

The following morning we started all over again, walking in a single line, but the speed at which we moved was more than the usual one. The boils on my right leg gave me a limp and I had to try and catch up with the one in front of me and bridge the gap. Major Lagira asked me what was the matter with my leg. I told him about the boil, and he called for his first aid kit and gave me two tetracycline capsules to put directly on my wound. He also asked me whether I would be able to walk since the journey that we had started was a long one. I did not give him any response because during that period when the LRA rebels asked any recruit whether he or she wanted to rest, if the answer was positive, then the person was to be killed straight away. The best thing to do to avoid shortening your life was to say that you are fit to go ahead to do anything that they have asked of you even if you have been given a load that is too heavy for you.

So I continued moving, but in pain because the sun was hot. He even hurt me the more when he said that the boils that were developing on my leg were because I was thinking of escaping. This was termed as 'no movement,' which showed itself in the form of boils in the arch of the feet or any part of the body, a sign that a new member in the LRA was worried or thinking of deserting the rebel group. This was true, but I felt the pain I was undergoing was more than I could withstand. The whole of that day we were only moving in the jungle with no hope of seeing any homestead, though I had the chance to see all sorts of vegetation and various landscapes. It was as though the base was far away but we would find ourselves reaching it so fast because of the constant speed that we were moving at.

After moving for two days, I noticed we had moved a long distance and in risky areas where at times soldiers would line up and advance towards whoever they got in the jungle. One morning they caught some hunters and took all their smoked game meat which they were not even going to eat. I felt so bad, especially in the morning when we moved through thick bushes with tall, sharp-bladed grass. The first people to take the lead would get wet from the morning dew, and it was cold as the wet grass brushed on our garments and made them wet and even tear away.

Majority of the people moving looked so shabby and ragged, with unkempt hair, limping with extremely heavy loads on their heads. I felt pity on one man who was given almost forty kilograms of beans to carry and expected to move at the same pace with other people. The load affected his neck and it looked as if his neck was bent due to the heavy load. It became unbearable for him so he dropped the heavy load and together with his friend they both took off backwards following the trail. This act was like an abomination to the

LRA. Immediately they stopped everyone and selected a few soldiers to follow the men. Resting from walking in the hot sun, I listened with a lot of pain in my heart as Major Lagira ordered for the murder of the two men who fled. In my heart, I was quietly praying for the men not to be found since they were being mistreated and overloaded. It was sad news to me to hear those who followed the men report that they had caught the men and killed them as ordered.

The murder of those two men, coupled with the gunshots that I heard behind us, scared and discouraged me from continuing with my escape plan as it would have lead to the loss of my life, so my friend and I decided not to escape until we were given the chance to come back to Uganda. From then on, I developed the attitude of perseverance toward any hardship that came my way, most especially moving long distances without water or stopping to rest, or even sleeping on an empty stomach. What mattered to me most then was my life and how I should take care of it. Every other day as we walked to Sudan there was at least one recruit or more being tortured either because they could no longer walk due to blisters on their legs or because they could no longer carry heavy loads given to them. The unlucky ones whose legs could not carry them any more were killed, most especially the boys.

Having moved for two good days without coming across any water source, we were informed that there was a river ahead of us called Atebi. It had a very strong current and was risky to cross in certain seasons and at times, the Sudanese People's Liberation Army (SPLA) would be hunting in the wilderness and any time they came into contact with the LRA, a serious exchange of gun fire took place because they were enemies. So when I heard we were to cross this dangerous river, I became so worried about what my fate would be and at the same time happy that I would quench my thirst. Having spent two days without nursing my wound due to lack of water, my leg was hurting so bad and had swollen to nearly double its size. I also felt that this was caused by the medicine Lagira had given me to treat the wound, that it wasn't the right medicine.

From the actions of the LRA soldiers, I saw that the majority were illiterate and ignorant, though I did not show them what I felt about what I saw them do. I was surprised to see some of the soldiers, especially young ones, using facial creams as toothpaste, sanitary towels as plaster and another carrying a whole bag of cement thinking it was a packet of baking flour.

On the fourth day, it was predicted that we would reach the river at around midday, so everyone tried his or her best to move faster. I was among the first ten people to reach the river. Luckily the crossing point was not as deep as I had feared. It was calm and only reached one's waist, so I took the chance to cross. I slowly lowered myself into the water but unfortunately I stepped on a slippery rock. The current took me a few metres away as I was weak, and I thought that would be my last time to see the bright sun again. In the process, other abductees who hadn't crossed started shouting for my rescue and one commander, whose name I did not know, helped me out of the river.

I felt so scared since what happened reminded me of the danger of that river that I was foretold. I struggled to get out but I didn't know how to swim, instead I moved forward in the direction of the water current, but I was relieved when I was rescued. Saving those who were drowning depended on the personality, availability and the skills of the swimmer. If the incident occurred at the time when those who were able to rescue were around, then the victim would be rescued irrespective of the period at which one was taken to the bush or abducted. When it came to drowning, any one is capable of doing so regardless of whether they were an original or a new recruit. Most people expressed their fear when it came to crossing the Atebi River, especially during the rainy season when the river was rough. It could even sweep away the best swimmers with its strong current after renewing its erosive power from its tributaries.

After crossing the river, we moved for a mile and Major Lagira gave an order stating that we would stay there for an hour while people prepared a simple meal for themselves since there was water, and after that the journey would continue. The first thing I did was to look for water and boil it for nursing my wound as its condition was worrying me a lot. The meal prepared was called *lugwiri*. These were small green seeds, which were first roasted and then boiled to make a sauce. We ate it plain without salt and the journey continued through thick, tall, rough grass for the rest of the day while heading towards the First River Kit, which was to be crossed the next day at around 9 am.

This was a huge river with a sand bed and cle[...]
We stopped for a while and took baths because the w[...]
clear. We later went ahead to the main road that goes[...]
I could not imagine walking comfortably on a road again after
nearly two months. While in Uganda, just to cross a main
road was a tug of war. It was a matter of life and death as you
tried to avoid the UPDF.

The first defense we reached in Sudan belonged to Arabs
(the Sudanese Armed Forces). These were a mixture of light
skinned and dark people. I had not seen the Arabs physically
before, except in movies like *The Jewels of the Nile*. I also learnt
about them in history at school. The little I knew about them
was that they participated in the development of the East
African coast and slave trade, and that they spoke Arabic. I
also got to know that they loved trade of any nature. They
seemed surprised and amused by our arrival and the only
words I could understand when they talked were *anyaka gorilla*
*(girl gorillas)* as they called ladies who were among the LRA.
The name gorilla came as a result of how the LRA behaves,
living in the bush, leading a harsh life like the gorilla, the ape.
*Anyaka* means a girl in my language. By using this term, they
were referring to all the females who were among the rebels.
According to what I think, the phrase *anyaka gorilla* was used
because it looked so strange to the Arabs for ladies to become
soldiers and live in such harsh conditions that are only fit for
men. They did not have female soldiers among their ranks.

We went ahead following the road that seemed unending
with many small stones that were painful to walk on, barefoot.
So many other recruits had no shoes. I had the sandals that

had been given to me earlier, but they were small, so my heels were touching the ground and I could feel how rough the road was. We passed three Arab defenses and reached a big bridge of the Second Kit River. Near the bridge, there were small grass thatched houses and within them were a few Arab soldiers all speaking in Arabic, holding long guns that I had never seen before. When I asked what kind of guns they were, as they looked so different from the ones the LRA were using, they told me that they were G3 guns. Another thing I saw was a military tank, which they called *adibaba*. As we proceeded, I kept on asking when we would finally reach the LRA defense as I was already tired of the never-ending journey. I was told to be patient and continue moving.

It was not until the next day at around 9 am that we finally arrived in Aruu, the LRA base. The day before, when we reached the main road, I saw a pick-up coming with two people and a few bodyguards in it, I was shocked to hear the girls around saying, "*Lapwony Madit* has come." They seemed to adore that *lapwony Madit* a lot. *Lapwony* means 'teacher', a term used to refer to commanders in the LRA. *Madit* meant 'the big one' or 'the supreme one'. I asked who *Lapwony Madit* was. Most people were both excited and showing respect to them. I was told that the person driving was Kony and the co-driver was Raska Lukwiya, one of the brigade commanders. I wondered whether it was the boss to drive the junior or vice versa, as Kony looked so much simpler than I had thought he would.

I began to think of the orders he had given to Major Lagira: *"Major Lagira, make sure you bring those girls safely and without mistreating them in any way."* I had mistaken Kony for the dark person, Raska Lukwiya, who was slim and dark with red eyes and looked cruel and arrogant. But Kony, who was the one driving, looked so friendly! I reflected on what he had said and thought that maybe they were going to sell us to the Arabs at a higher price since we had arrived in good condition, but that was not the case. On reaching the LRA camp in Aruu, I noticed that there were very many people who lived independently from the Sudanese soldiers. Even after we had stayed for a while, no one went missing except for those who died of cholera or in the front line, though the living conditions were very poor with limited water supply, food shortage, and misery due to mistreatment from the originals. Most recruits lacked any clothing and were dressed in rags.

Before my abduction I had heard rumours that the LRA exchanged the abducted people for guns with Arabs, just as it had been done historically during the East African long distance trade, but that was not the case. I never ever saw anyone being exchanged for anything with the Arabs. Instead Joseph Kony advised those who had been abducted not to seek refuge from the Arabs because they have the mentality of slavery but rather stay within the LRA. So, eventually I came to a conclusion that the main reason the LRA abducted people was for them to get enough manpower. But if some were sold or exchanged, then the number of the LRA would not have been that high. There were approximately 5,000 or more people, excluding those who were in Uganda and those who were dying on the frontline and of diseases and starvation.

# 4

# Arrival in Sudan

*"It was unfortunate that I was in the hands of the very people who took me out of school."*

We arrived in Sudan at the LRA main camp, Aruu, at 9 am in the morning. It was the 12th of December, 1996. Everyone I saw seemed so excited about our arrival, except for the weak recruits who seemed to have no interest or energy to line by the roadside to watch the new abductees arrive. We saw people who had been abducted before us and other LRA members lining along the road, waiting to see the newly abducted. As for us, we proceeded to the main camp. Whenever any new lot of new recruits were entering the LRA base, the originals would stand along the road to see them, in the hope of seeing someone they knew or a relative, so as to inquire how their loved ones in Uganda were doing. What I noticed was that they kept on commenting in terms of beauty, ugliness and sympathy, and others would rejoice that at least the number of people joining them in the world of misery was increasing. In December 1997, I too waited along the roadside to see new people arrive in the hope of seeing anyone from my home area, but there was no one.

After entering Aruu, we stopped at a big field next to the operation room where all the military activities took place. It was a very bright morning, the sun was shining so brightly in a cloudless sky. This reminded me of my old good days at school. However, it was unfortunate that I was in the hands of the very people who took me out of school, where I thought I would realise my dream and wipe away the idea of sectarianism between girls and boys that I witnessed in my primary school and society.

With the constant movement both day and night without resting for nearly two months and being in constant fear, I badly needed a place where I could stay for a while without moving. So I was glad to have reached Sudan where I at least rested, though what was ahead of me was unpredictable. On arrival in the field, we were handed over to the operation room (where all military decisions were made and executed) together with other items like grains, beans, and goats collected in raids in Uganda and carried by new recruits to Sudan where they were distributed to people who had not gone to Uganda for the operation: pigeon peas, smoked meat, and sim-sim (sesame seeds). We, the Aboke girls, found ourselves among the goods looted for the LRA. Other soldiers we had walked with disappeared to their usual homes/positions in Aruu.

The LRA had a headquarters called Control Altar, and four other small brigades. The first one was Stockree, then Sinia and Gilva. The spirits that guided Joseph Kony named each Brigade. All these brigade names had different meanings, which were related to situations that occured in the LRA. The fourth one was called Twinkle. It was the last brigade to be formed and it mainly comprised of Kony's security guards; his chief of security was the brigade commander. It was Major Lagira's group-commanders from Stockree - that had abducted us from our school and handed us over to the operation room in Sudan that is in control altar, the central ruling body. It is the place where all policies were made, and the central body that governed the whole LRA. It comprised of Kony who was the central authority, followed by field commanders, then chief-of-staffs and then heads of departments, like chief defense, yard, medical department, administration block, and support.

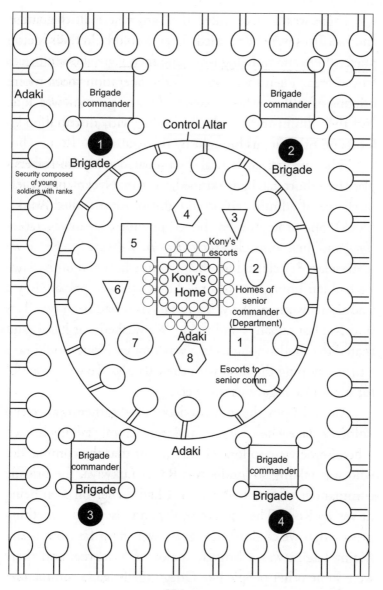

*LRA camp*

There was a place called the Yard where all the rituals and sacrifices were performed. They would hold their special prayers here and only high-ranking men were allowed in the fenced area. Then there was also the operation room where briefing of soldiers who were going for an operation was done and the administration block, dealing with distribution of food and other items brought by the Arabs.

When we arrived, a meal was prepared at Nyeko Tolbert's place by a short, fat, light-skinned, woman. Nyeko Tolbert was in charge of administration in Control Altar (called Admin Block). She brought a few boiled potatoes, green vegetables (*boo*) and then some okra (*otigolwoka*). We were fifteen, so we made a large circle and for the first time in two months since we had left home, we ate a meal that was well prepared by a traditional woman. We were hungry as it had been two days since we last ate any solid food. We washed our hands and shared the food among us in a way that each one would take a turn scooping the food with their hands. We were grateful for it because it gave us some energy.

Around 1 pm, the commanders started gathering at Nyeko Tolbert's place where we were and were happily talking to each other. Some were so loud. I later learnt that the commander who was talking so loudly was Raska Lukwiya, the brigade commander of Stockree, whom I had earlier on seen being driven by Kony. They became quiet and discussed something private that we couldn't hear as we were a bit far from them. Major Lagira was a brigade major of Stockree, and there were some other people like Odego, the brigade commander of Gilva.

I felt disgusted because they seemed to be so happy and yet I wanted freedom. I felt like they were looking at us with lustful eyes and yet they were far too old to be our husbands. In fact as I saw it, they were the ages of our fathers. I also realised that Nyeko Tolbert knew me and recognised me, as he narrated to me that he once worked with my dad before he joined LRA, so he mentioned my dad's name and where they worked together. But I wasn't happy to meet him again because I felt that if he really knew my father, he would have been the one to get me out of the life of captivity. Instead, his first remarks on our arrival were so disturbing. He said, "Welcome to the land of paradise. This is where we enjoy life and I hope you will enjoy too." What Nyeko Tolbert said was in contrast to what I saw. The place was dry and the sun was so hot. The people I saw at first, especially the boys, were all skinny and were wearing combats that were ragged and old. They were slow in their movements and had no sign of hope in them. It showed starvation, mistreatment and no freedom at all, especially in the *adaki* (trenches dug all around the perimeter of an army barracks that were used for hiding in case of an attack) where recruits were forced to stay. Each soldier had his own *adaki*. In the LRA, the *adaki* was at the edge of all the brigades that surrounded the headquarters. All the boys were always positioned at night in the *adaki* for security. There was a difference that I noticed between the boys in the *adaki* and those who were chosen as bodyguards. It was mainly on the issue of food. Those at the *adaki* were served food in one dish which they shared with those on duty as bodyguards. Luckily the bodyguards on many occasions would have access to the food their commander left after eating at the *adaki*, which made the bodyguards healthier and look better than the *adaki* boys who were thin, dirty and malnourished.

Some people, most of whom were new arrivals, developed lice on their hair and bodies and in their clothes because of inaccessibility of adequate soap, water and poor hygiene. This was typical for the *adaki* boys. To make matters worse, the spirits that speak to Joseph Kony had given an order that no one in the LRA should cut his or her hair. He said a person's strength was in his or her hair, like Samson's from the Bible. This really favoured the breeding of these parasitic animals. The boys had lice more than the girls because they were not interested in keeping their bodies clean. It got to a point where the lice's eggs could be seen in vast numbers in their hair.

At around 5 pm at Nyeko Tolbert's place, I saw the bodyguards to the commanders who had earlier gathered there, coming one at a time and being given one of the school girls to go with. We had no say. We didn't know where we were going to be taken but had to follow whoever we were asked to go with for the sake of our lives. We knew that these people could kill us any time if we failed to obey what they said. Some were kind but others were not, although when it came to obeying orders from their commanders, there was no mercy. I think what really calmed us to some extent from the time of our abduction was the order that Joseph Kony gave about us not being mistreated. His instructions to treat us well made us believe that we would be released at some point.

It was around 6 pm when my turn came, I asked the escort who came to get me in my local language, where he was taking me. He said that he had been sent to take me to where he stays at 'Johns', a senior commander in the LRA. Upon reaching, I saw about four grass-thatched houses and a very huge mango tree in the courtyard. There was an old man seated on a hammock-like chair relaxing, and that was 'John'. I didn't bother to greet him and instead went and entered a small hut which was a kitchen. I wondered whether a person of such an old age also existed in the LRA because I had not seen such an old person in the last almost two months that I had spent among them.

I was also greeted by a young girl who was about 9 years old, and I kept pondering whether she was born there or just abducted at such an early age. I kept quiet in that small hut as I kept on looking all around, trying to figure out how life was going to be in this new environment. I had no idea whether I was going to be given to the old man as a wife or not. After a while, a tall and thin lady who was the old man's first wife, Betty, came carrying a jerrycan of water on her head. He called her and she went to him after putting the water down. She was told to give me a dress to change into as I was still wearing my school sweater, which was so dirty. She was also instructed to boil some water for nursing my wound. She entered the hut where I was and greeted me as is culturally practised with a visitor. She then quickly warmed water and told me to go and bathe. I did and my leg was nursed. After washing my hair, my head started itching terribly from the effect of the lice. I got them from one of the girls with whom I shared a bedsheet with while in Uganda. The effect of the lice on my head nearly prevented me from falling asleep that night.

The next morning I was woken by a woman who had a baby and wanted to light a fire to make some porridge for her baby. I got up confused and did not know what to do not even who to ask for some water to clean my face. I observed that time and again whoever was passing John would stamp their feet and salute him while saying, *"Ki pwo Rwot, Lapwony!"* (Praise the Lord, teacher!) And he would respond *"Ki pwo naka-naka"*(praise the Lord forever). This was a common greeting to the commanders by the junior soldiers. Later, I was given some grains of dura millet to grind in preparation for lunch that day. I did it since I had learnt how to grind at my grandmother's place when I was still in the village. Following the method that my grandmother taught me to grind millet, I was given about three and a half kilograms of dura millet, which is equivalent to seven cups, I could not move for long distances to fetch water due to my painful leg. Since work had to be shared, that was my part for the day.

As it is done bit by bit, I added the dura millet on the big grinding stone while moving the stone to and fro to make the flour. It was difficult as I had taken years without grinding and more so, I had been given a lot of grains to grind. My palms started hurting so I paused for a while and looked at it as it had started turning red. I had no choice  so I continued until I finished. Other people completed their part of the work. I only waited for the meal but with additional pain since my leg also had painful wounds, and this time around, my hands were paining, too. At least I got some relief from the constant movement to Sudan.

Using the flour I made, bread was mingled and the sauce was prepared. The sauce, which looked so funny, was served in one dish, but I could not imagine what kind of ingredients had been used to make it. It was brown in color, with a mixture of black substances and slippery when touched but later I was told the sauce was made out of preserved okra that was grounded into powder, later mixed with water and boiled the way porridge is made with a taste of pepper in it. The seven of us all gathered around one dish after washing our hands and prayed, and as soon as the prayer was over, we started to eat. I could not cope with the speed at which my colleagues ate and I only had the chance to have three bites of the entire meal. I didn't know that ladies also struggle over food and eat that fast, since I was used to our ways of eating from school, where each one would be served in her own plate, and food was slowly eaten with dignity. I began to wonder how I was going to cope and survive in that place. But I later got used to it. As the saying goes, behave like Romans when in Rome. For the first two weeks, I would only grab food twice and then sit to watch the rest eat as I got ashamed of them struggling for food. To me it looked weird to swallow food without chewing well and then rushing for more. It was survival for the fittest because food was very scarce and the best use of what was there was made. This struggle for food was even worse for the newly abducted.

Later in the evening on the second day in Sudan, John called all the ladies who were living in his home and told them that I would be staying in his home. At the time, I did not understand he meant that I would be living there as his wife.

He went on to say that I should only interact with the four older women in his home and not the two young girls who had been brought to act as babysitters to his wives. I was not comfortable with what he said because I felt that the women were older than me, so I had nothing in common to discuss with them. Secondly, my mum had taught me not to stay with those who are older than me because they can mislead me. It was not easy for me to adjust to this new system. And all that was going on was so confusing to me. To worsen the situation, the following morning, Joseph Kony and his two other brigade commanders came to brief me on the same issue.

Normally, when recruits were brought, they would be distributed to the commanders who were willing to take care of them. For the boys, they were trained as soldiers. They were also expected to do domestic work like sweeping the compound and clearing the garden, and the commander taking care of them would call them his sons. He was to provide them with food, uniforms and ensure that they are well fed and healthy, but would submit them in case they were needed for military work. For the girls, older ones were taken as wives according to the wish of the commanders. The young ones were kept until they began their first menstruation periods, then they were given as wives strictly to those with ranks. It was not permitted for a man to run after every woman he sees, instead they were restricted to only those who were rightfully given to them from the operation room. Failure to do that amounted to death as their standing order stated that adultery was punishable by death.

## Life in Aruu: December 1996 – April 1997

I was given as a wife to John, who was one of the top commanders, six days later. They first conducted a ceremony called *wir* or cleansing whereby a messenger went around the camp informing the new people to report to the yard for the ceremony. The yard was a sacred place where the LRA would pray and perform their rituals. It was divided into two sections. The inside one was strictly for men and it was an abomination for a woman to enter there. This was well fenced to prevent women from entering it. I went for the ceremony and ladies were the first to be initiated followed by men. Once again we were told to remove our blouses and make a circle with bare chests as the controllers (the men in charge of performing the ceremony) sang the same common Christian songs, which we knew from home. We were even invited to sing along with them but it was so embarrassing for me as our breasts were uncovered and even the men who were conducting the ceremony could see us. One person was using a calabash to sprinkle a special kind of water that was mixed with a white powdery substance known as 'camouflage' and drops of shea nut oil, on everyone.

When that was done, Shea oil was smeared on our foreheads, chests, backs, palms, the back of our hands and lastly our feet. The third step was to make the signs of the heart on our chests using an egg, which was dipped in camouflage and was supposed to reveal whether the anointed person was sick so as to cure any illnesses and for protection. We had to remain with this on our chest for three days, that meant no bathing while observations were made on the shape of the heart drawn on the chest using camouflage. If it disappeared before the three days were over, then this showed that one was sick. When it remained for the three days, it showed that one was healthy. This was where commanders who had interest in certain girls would judge and make the necessary steps in making the girls their wives.

Whoever resisted a commander's proposal for sex after she had been given as a wife to that commander was severely punished. A case in point was one person who was a neighbour to us. She told me that she was given to a deaf and dumb man but she refused. Consequently, she was seriously beaten using a red hot machete thrice on her back, which left her with serious wounds but still, she was supposed to stay with him.

When we reached Sudan, we were warned that we had already caused enough trouble for the LRA so failure to follow what they told us would lead to the loss of our lives, as they had done before with other students they had abducted before us. So all of us were given off by force to rebel commanders as wives.

In Aruu there was a water crisis, so people were forced to walk long distances to fetch water. If you went for water around 7 am, you would come back at about 11 am because the water was scarce even at the well. It had to be fetched from a seasonal river that was so deep in the valley, one had to dig holes using metallic dishes through the sand in the river bed to get the water. It would come out slowly and the demand was high. When coming back from the well, one had to climb a very steep hill, which was difficult while carrying twenty litre jerrycan on one's head. This made it challenging for everyone to use the water freely since it was insufficient and very difficult to reach. Because of this, I witnessed a three litre jerrycan of water being given to a group of 20 boys to take after a meal that was not adequate at all. The faster you could grab the better. Those who missed could do nothing but suffer without water to quench their thirst. This experience was so strange to me because I had never known in my life that food and water were struggled for. I felt ashamed when I saw commanders mediating matters to do with food and water. Such minor issues should have been resolved by junior commanders. Girls refused to give water to the boys because it was so scarce. This created a lot of bitterness among women, men, boys and girls in the camp to the point that the boys lamented that even if they found any girl wounded during battle, they would not offer any help.

I remember I was given another task to pick vegetables (*boo*) from a garden, which almost had no vegetables and yet that was the only source. This became my task every day, both mornings and evenings. I was to go to the same field every morning to pick vegetables. But the quantity I found kept on reducing as it takes time to grow in the absence of rain. It was also not given enough time to grow because that garden was the only source of vegetables. It was hard to pick enough for the entire household, which had 27 people in total.

Consequently, finding food became a problem. We resorted to wild plants that were only found along the rivers which meant that every woman had to compete to grab enough for her 'family.' I later realised that the people who had been abducted earlier on in that position, the LRA defense, had cultivated a few food crops like small green peas (*lugwiri/coroko*) and groundnuts, but the groundnuts were being kept as seeds for the next planting season. Unfortunately, all these things were left untouched after we were attacked by the combined troops of the Uganda People's Defense Forces (UPDF) and the Sudanese People's Liberation Army (SPLA) on the 9th of April 1997.

The main reason for cultivation by the LRA was to obtain food to support the ever-increasing number of abductees that could not be sustained with the little food donation that was being given by the Sudanese government. The inadequate food supply resulted in starvation and malnourishment of many young boys and girls who ended up dying in large numbers.

For a period of about four months, from mid-December 1996 to early-April 1997, which I spent in Aruu, all new captives were involved in various military activities such as learning how to dismantle and reassemble a machine gun and the names of various parts of a gun like the trigger, the magazine, and generally how a gun works, alongside marching and saluting. Later, guns were distributed. Though given a gun for nearly six months, not even once did I shoot it or take part in any military activity. However, I was to carry it whenever I was going out of the barracks. It was even worse when it came to fetching water from a water source that was very far away. With the weight of a twenty litre jerrycan on my head, I felt the additional weight of the gun was a burden but I had no option as everyone had to carry one. Sometimes when I was walking in the hot sun to fetch water and happened to see an aircraft flying over the sky heading to Juba, I would wish to hold its wings so that I could fly away from the miserable life I was living among the LRA. I thought again of escaping, but I imagined the long distance between Sudan and Uganda, and I gave up because of fear of getting lost in the wilderness. Besides that, I was not so familiar with directions and on our way to Sudan, there came a point where we were only rotating around without any clear direction which caused confusion on how to return to Uganda.

While still in Aruu, my new foster family and I even carried out cultivation of crops like millet and sorghum that were meant to increase food supply. This was just a warm-up but the real cultivation was ahead. It was not easy for me even though I used to do a bit of weeding in our school garden every evening after classes.

During this period, we woke up to go to the field as early as 5 am and sometimes earlier than that when it was very cold. Sometimes I felt like remaining in bed but it was an order for everyone to go digging. On leaving the LRA defense, we entered deep into the bush where we dug. This involved getting wet because of the cold morning dew, and by the time we reached the garden we were shivering as our clothes would be wet. This morning dew contributed a lot to the tearing of our few clothes.

From the garden, the field measurements would be made for each one both horizontally and vertically then the actual digging begin. This would take about six to eight hours till the sun was hot and everyone would be hungry and thirsty. We would leave the garden to go back home between midday and 2 pm, when we were completely exhausted. Despite the fatigue, women/girls had to carry back home bundles of firewood for future use. We would go back home only to get little food that could not replace the energy lost. As a result, I grew very thin. Those who did digging as part of their profession before their abduction were lucky while this was a torture to me and others who only held the hoe occasionally. It was so unfortunate that we did not live to enjoy what we sweated for. Combined forces of Ugandan soldiers and the SPLA attacked us in April 1997 and drove us out of Aruu to Jebelen, Nicitu, Rubangatek, and eventually Binrwot where we did the same or more cultivation for sustenance. This was because food donations from the Khartoum government were no more due to the misunderstandings between the government and the LRA.

Cutting grass for roofing houses was yet another activity that I did before we fled from Aruu. I had never cut grass before, not even from home. We used a sickle to cut a particular type of grass that grew to the height of about two metres. The grass was cut, organised and heaped in bundles big enough then tied. We then carried it on the head and took it home. What I hated most was how the rough blades of grass worked on the skin, especially the arms. During cutting, the sharp blades would come into contact with my arms while gathering, most especially when the sun was hot. This would leave wounds that hurt when washing and permanent dark scars on the skin.

One day, two of the women whom I was staying with had a serious quarrel that was later brought before their commander. He ended up punishing not only them but all seven ladies in the 'home', and each person had to present thirty bundles of grass in just three days. To me it was a burden. If cutting only one bundle that I started with was too much for me, how about thirty? Not to mention that the source of the grass was far away from the defense. Every morning we woke up and went wandering in the wilderness far away from the defense in search of grass. I managed to cut about ten bundles, before we were told to stop.

In the first three months that I spent in Sudan, I noticed one big difference that existed between the females and the males that had no ranks or the recruits. I first noticed this from the assembly ground that was known as the church. This was where Joseph Kony briefed everyone on how the LRA works. He also gave orders and updates on what was taking place in Uganda and what was being done by either the LRA or the UPDF. This was how LRA politics was instilled in the minds of new captives.

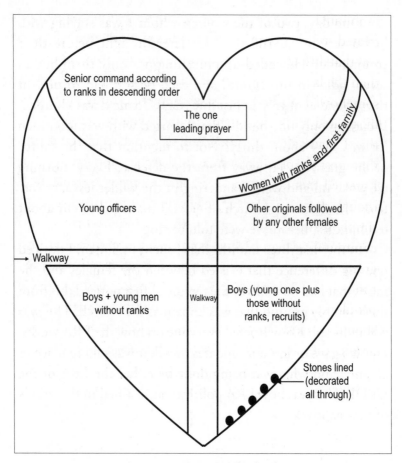

*Seating arrangement at the church*

From the seating arrangement in the church, the highly ranked army officers sat in front, followed by those with low ranks and behind them those without ranks. A wide space was left between ladies and men to avoid contact. On the other side, a few men with ranks sat, followed by women who were *originals* and lastly recruits who were girls. Mixing up was highly prohibited. When it came to treatment in homes, boys were treated well in comparison to ladies. I wondered why there was that difference. Maybe because the boys were more active than the ladies when it came to military activities. I became somehow disturbed as I saw energetic young boys being mistreated and consequently dying. One other observation that I made after spending only a few days in the camp is that most people there were not friendly. I noticed that when I greeted them, a response was given but with reluctance as though there is a grudge. They would sometimes keep quiet, simply glare or mutter. I saw this as rudeness since in the community where I come from such a response after one is greeted means something is wrong. It puzzled me for some time until I realised that it was because of the miserable life people were living in LRA. Yet in my mind, such a grudge should be held between captives and captors, and not exist among the captives. Everyone was bitter with everyone else.

# 5

# Norms in the LRA

*"There was no time that the LRA had total peace."*

## Dressing

Ladies were only allowed to wear long skirts without slits, which did not expose parts of their bodies like the thighs or legs, emphasising decency. The clothes one was captured wearing were burned. This also matched what happened at home on return, where the things one returned with from the bush like clothes were also destroyed by burning. This signified the beginning of a new life.

I was given an African-design dress that was long, black in color, and had a design of a hen with eggs. This was my second dress. When one was washed, I wore the other one. Clothes were usually raided   from Uganda and brought to Sudan. So getting clothes was hard for those who were not allowed to go to Uganda, as the case was for me and all the schoolgirls that were abducted from St Mary's College Aboke. We were banned from returning to Uganda, as they believed we would escape. This deprived me of the only chance that

I thought was left for my freedom because for one to escape from Sudan alone was a very high risk.

Materials (fabrics, polyester, nylon, cotton) were made into clothes by local tailors, who had learned to sew on their own. I also learnt how to make dresses out of the materials. This was in 1998 after one tailor had made the wrong design that was contrary to what I wanted and even misused the material. So I decided to undo what she had made and sewed it again using my own skills. I learnt how she cut it, and I kept on practicing in small pieces until I could make perfect dresses, skirts, blouses, trousers and shirts.

During my last years in captivity, I had become a professional tailor and other people brought their new materials to me to be made into dresses and skirts. Even some of Kony's wives brought their materials to me to sew. This kept me busy and won me fame and respect. The most important people in my life then were the ladies who brought their materials for me to sew. Personally, I felt good that I was using my natural talent to serve those who needed my service. Again, I was able to do something that was unique. Though I was not paid directly, the kind clients would give me the remaining pieces of cloth. I believe my clients felt confident and smart wearing outfits that were presentable at that level of the bush. However, I was not the only tailor. Others were there though the ladies looked for an outstanding service. Tailoring was part of my life from 1998 to 2004, when I escaped from the LRA.

Joseph Kony used to criticise how people dressed in Uganda. He said they are indecent, especially those who wore tight trousers or short skirts with long slits. He said that it is a sign of immorality, and he blamed it for the spread of HIV/AIDS in Uganda. He believed that the already abducted people were a new race of people who he termed Acholi 'A' and those who are still back in Uganda were Acholi 'B', since those who were in Uganda were going to perish of HIV/AIDS as a result of immorality. He believed that the strict Standing Orders that existed in the LRA against immorality would help prevent the LRA from dying of AIDS. The LRA looked at themselves as superior and a well-cultured group of people in comparison to those who were living in Uganda.

**Food**

I realised there was shortage of food. The Sudanese used to donate food but it was inadequate to sustain the ever increasing population of LRA soldiers. In the process of looking for something to fill their empty stomachs, they ate wild fruits that made their bodies swell, leading to their death. They ate fruits like *ogali*, a tree species in the jungle that I used to shake as a musical instrument when playing with my cousin sisters while living at my grandmother's place.

**Initiations**

For children born in captivity there were no special rites performed although, naming was either done by Joseph Kony or by the parents depending on the conditions or circumstances under which a child was born. I underwent two initiations in Uganda immediately following my abduction.

The very first one was to be anointed with shea nut butter. The second initiation I underwent was a practical one that took place after about three weeks from the time we were abducted. It took place in a different area, as we were always on the move from village to village. We were gathered, made a circle and the controllers, those who were going to perform the initiation, sung their songs, especially religious songs as they sprinkled water using calabashes on us using a special leaf known as *obokeolwedo*. The second step was smearing the forehead, chest, back, palms and the feet with shea oil. The third step was smearing a white substance that was mixed with water and shea butter on our backs and chests using hands, tracing a shape of a heart.

The last stage was an instruction that we should stay bare chested for three days and nights without bathing. This bothered us most, especially staying bare-chested, because it was an embarrassment to do so in front of the males in the community. This made the commander who was guarding us in our position give an order to the junior soldiers to make sure that none of us left the tent that night, not even to go for even short calls as this might be an attempt to escape following the initiation ceremony. It was excessively dark that night as it had rained and the weather was cloudy. He decided to tighten the security because he saw how unhappy we were as we thought after the initiation we may not be released. It was extremely hard for one to escape from the rebels unless carefully planned, after pleading with a lot of humility to God to grant them courage to do so. We had all gathered together wondering about the implication of the initiation, saying whatever these people did would not make us be like them. We were determined to go back home even if they performed all these rituals on us.

I remember following the second initiation, Captain Oyet sent for me at night. I went but was extremely scared as it was late in the night and not appropriate for me to be alone in his tent where he was to sleep. I thought he had the idea of persuading and later forcing me to become his wife, since he had contributed a lot to my remaining in the bush, and maybe this was the best time he had to talk to me. He told me to sit down and I did. He called me by my surname and said, "I was supposed to beat all these five girls except you because they are showing us that we are primitive by their actions and they are educated by criticising us, but I have not seen that in you. And if you go ahead with your good character, you will never have problems in the LRA until the day you will return to your people. Only simple people like you can stay and survive here."

Then I went back and told my friends what he had told me as there was need for them to change their behavior in regard to what the commander was complaining about. Later Captain Oyet called the six of us who were in his position and told us the same thing. "Starting from today, all of you should forget that you are students and all you should do is to behave like soldiers. You ceased being students on the 10th of October and that's the end." He was trying to pinpoint my friends, trying to correct them, and then he told us to go but still we had that fear in our hearts. Why were they guarding us like that? We had no intention of escaping at that time because we knew we would be released as our Deputy Headmistress

Sister Rachelle had promised. So we cautioned ourselves that no one should even attempt to escape as this would risk our chance of being freed. It was better for all to stay than one of us escaping and leaving the remaining girls to die.

There was a special kind of shiny stone that at times was given to everyone to keep without losing. Everyone was to find a way of making sure they had the stone all the time by sewing it into a piece of material and wearing it like a bracelet or necklace for protection. Sometimes everyone was ordered to carry blessed water (this was water brought from the yard that had been mixed with shea butter and blessed) with them wherever they moved. It was kept in small bottles that were hung around the neck using strings until we were told to remove them by Joseph Kony's spirit. As explained to us, this was for protection against the enemy. When crossing a big river, everyone had to fetch water using their hands and sprinkle it on their heads following a sign of the cross, which was another sign of protection.

After the initiation ceremony I was so scared that if I put on my clothes before the three days were over, I would either die or something bad would happen to me because I didn't know anything about the ceremony. According to what was explained to us by some of the *originals*, those who disobeyed the instructions of such ceremonies were often hit by bullets in case of any attack and died, this scared me so much. The LRA was trying all possible ways to make us part of them. I also felt like they were deeply tied to spiritual beliefs as they had so many rules and carried so many sacred objects. All these rituals remained a mystery to me as I failed to understand their exact meanings. I participated because I was in the same boat as them and I had no option. Worst of all it was an order and so any disobedience would result in punishment.

Between 2001 and 2002, Joseph Kony ordered everyone in the LRA be cleansed by dipping themselves in River Kit (this was a seasonal river in the then Southern Sudan where LRA camped along the banks) once in a month. One was to wake up very early in the morning and rush to River Kit as a family to dip themselves into the water four times while praying to God, pleading for anything they wanted him to do for them (*chant/incantation*). Others were in the form of sacrifices where a black sheep was slaughtered and the food that the sheep had eaten and was still undergoing digestion process (*wee*) was put on the path where everyone was to pass. This was an order from the spirits that controlled the LRA through Kony and the main reason was to overcome the occurrence of negative things like enemy attacks and bad luck. One time, only men were supposed to go for that ritual. It was supposed to be performed at midnight very far away from the LRA barracks. When they returned, I asked what happened there and I was told that the ritual was to remove all the evil spirits and demons that were causing problems like sicknesses in LRA. I was told that the participants were enclosed in strings during the ceremony, but there wasn't a clear explanation given to me for that. The voices of many people who were not physically seen were heard moving in the opposite direction, lamenting and complaining that they had been sent away, which made participants of the ceremony believe that the evil spirits were the ones fleeing. The participants were then ordered to come back quietly without looking back but one person insisted on looking back and became mad. Instructions were very important to follow. Failure to follow amounted to suffering the consequences.

## Dreams

Dreams in the LRA were always taken seriously and interpreted to mean something that would happen in the future. When someone dreamt that he or she swum in muddy water that was reddish brown in colour, it was interpreted that that person was likely to meet something bad in the nearby future. Another was when one dreamt that he or she ate meat in a dream; it was interpreted that somebody close to him or her would die.

If one ate ripe fruits in a dream, it was interpreted that there would be a shortage of food. I remember I also had a dream that I was competing with two other people in a swimming race in a pool of reddish brown water and I won. As I was reaching the end of the pool, I saw a muscular, hairy arm of a man stretched out to pick me out of the water. When I narrated this dream to John it was interpreted that an attack would happen but that I would survive it. The mighty hand that rescued me signified the help that was being given to me by the angels. It wasn't long before an attack took place and I survived. This made me believe in certain dreams, as mine was fulfilled.

Among the many dreams differently interpreted, one familiar one was when a person was beaten by rain in a dream. This dream was interpreted to mean that one would be shot by bullets. Whatever Kony said was strictly obeyed and people believed that it would happen. For example, he predicted war, peace, women's fertility and bad omens on people, and these things actually happened just the way it had been said.

Among the many predictions, the first one I learnt about was our abduction. Those who were already there in the LRA, the originals, narrated it to me. Kony said, "I have my 30 girls in a school, and through them, the whole world will get to know about the existence of the LRA as a powerful rebel group in Uganda. And in the process, LRA activity in northern Uganda will be known all over the world. Whatever will be done, the very girls who are meant for this place will not run away but they will get them there. Those that are not meant for this place will be taken back. This is to lift the name of our God so that you believe that whatever they say will happen." This was what Joseph Kony told the LRA community one year before we were abducted.

When there was war or a battle, there was plenty of food donated by the Sudanese government and no one complained of hunger. At times there were periods of sickness when other things like food and security were okay. Also at such periods, there were no conflicts among the people.

## Witchcraft

From 1998, people who practiced witchcraft of various kinds also existed. They were later punished by death. Some turned water from the well as red as blood. Others night danced naked around people's huts in order to divert their sickness to those who slept inside. There were also incidences where some people did things that made food not to get ready because the witches were earlier denied food or angered by the person targeted. For example, beans remained hard despite being cooked for a long time on a very hot fire. Others made their friends' stomachs swell and have diarrhea because of simple misunderstandings between them. These witches explained that they were given their powers by their grandparents, who were also witches.

They would enter a person's hut at night when the person was sleeping and practice their witchcraft, unknown to the person who was asleep. However much the person tried to come back to his or her senses, he or she would fail until the witch left. Without your knowledge you would find yourself doing extraordinary things like the witches did because you had been transformed into a witch.

Witchcraft affected everyone in the LRA. Even the children born in the bush that were so treasured died of witchcraft. Some witches admired a baby after carrying it and later the baby would die without having been sick. For adults, some suffered from stomach upsets. This practice was also used by the witches as a way of taking revenge on those who mistreated them.

Witches were comprised of men and young boys who were then known as *mony pa Kony* (child soldiers that were below fourteen years of age), women (two of whom were Kony's wives) and a young girl who was staying at his place, as well. One of Kony's wives (Christine) had two children, Wokorach, followed by a girl called Akwiya, who were also killed together with their mother because she had transformed them into witches. They said they would not waste their bullets on such people. That's why they were tortured to death. On many occasions when Christine was preparing meals for children in

Kony's home, she called her son Wokorach to first jump three times over the tray of food that was to be given to the children. Her co-wives became concerned and asked her to explain that to them, and she told them that it was an initiation ceremony for her children to join the world of witches.

Another of Kony's wives who was a witch confessed that she inherited witchcraft from her grandparents who were also witches, so her failure to practice caused sickness to her. She transferred the sickness that would have attacked her to other people by night dancing around them when she was naked, or swelling and becoming bigger than her usual size, or cutting people's hair and their pieces of garments for her use so as to cause problems for them. To add to the above, she also defecated by the doorway of one of the huts that belonged to her co-wives, and she was discovered. In some cultures in Africa such an act is an abomination for an adult. According to all that these two women and the others did on many occasions plus their confessions, they were found guilty of being witches.

At one point, so many cases of witchcraft were reported to the operation room that Joseph Kony ordered their arrest, and they were all killed. In my understanding, the practice of witchcraft increased from 1998 because this was a period when most of the LRA were based in Sudan without moving to Uganda, so hidden characteristics like witchcraft showed up because people were idle. After their arrest, the witches were forced to explain their practices. After a thorough investigation, they were found guilty. This first lot that was killed in 1998 was lucky enough to have missed being tortured before being killed. There were about twenty, most of who were from the Gilva brigade. The second lot was about 16 in number. This happened in 2002 during the 'Iron Fist' operation and they were brutally tortured. They were tied with ropes and dragged through rough areas with sharp stones, thorns and even tree stumps that caused injuries all over their bodies.

It was horrible to see them before they were finally killed. I saw them four days after they received their first punishment, and I could not believe that they were human beings. All their bodies were bruised with dark and red marks as a result of the rough materials they were forced to pass over. After seeing them, my whole body started aching. I became speechless and felt sorry for them because of their pain, but at the same time wished they were not witches.

Joseph Kony, had warned the witches that such practices were not allowed in the LRA, and I can remember him saying jokingly one day while addressing us that the witches should bear in mind that he is a super witch so they should not try his patience with witchcraft.

## Child soldiers

Children made up the majority of Kony's army. They were ruthless because they grew up to know, talk and act in aggressive ways and in bitterness. They mistreated the elderly people that were abducted after them. I saw one young soldier commanding a recruit old enough to be his father to kneel down and touch his chin while saying he respects the younger boy. They killed or tortured the elderly abductees for giving them little food or forced them to grind grains like millet and maize to make flour for preparing porridge. This was common with the soldiers who grew up in the bush.

They killed you if you said you were tired and wanted to rest. They asked you to go and rest under a tree and then kill you on arrival. I remember one kind original warned me not to admit that I was tired even if I was, so as to save my life.

Many child soldiers died due to hunger. They were given little food, and yet they had a lot of work to do. They patroled for long distances to loot food from the villages in Sudan and also fight at the same time. They needed a lot of food to replace the energy used. If a commander failed to monitor how the boys he was taking care of were being fed by his women, then he would lose all of them to starvation and diseases like cholera, or they would be transferred.

For example in Jebelen II in 1998, many new recruits arrived from Uganda. Some were even students, as I noticed from their language and character. Many died of hunger. Within just a week or so, they had lost a lot of weight and looked totally different from what they were before. I could not believe my eyes when I saw them disappearing one by one. The wives of the commanders who were supposed to take care of them fed these boys on *dura* (flour like sorghum that is used to prepare bread) that was not finely ground , which only increased their diarrhea. They used to stay only at the *adaki* area without anybody to care for them. At some point, the number of recruits outweighed the amount of food that was available and even those who were to take care of them were few in number and as such could not do it well. The excessive increase in the number of recruits was due to Joseph Kony's order to increase the number of LRA soldiers. When going to fetch water, I used to pass by the *adaki* where those suffering from cholera were isolated. I saw their suffering. When they died, their bodies were thrown away, not even given a proper burial. This happened a lot in April when there was a cholera outbreak. Sometimes shallow graves were dug for the remains of the boys. Animals dug them out and carried some parts away. Bones of the dead were scattered all over.

# 6

# Women in the LRA

*"The newly abducted girls were treated as slaves."*

On my arrival in the LRA community, I found ladies who had already stayed for over 8 years, who were awarded ranks. The highest rank was 2<sup>nd</sup> Lieutenant and they were given the title *'originals'*. They were the ones to guide the newly abducted, show them how they would survive in the LRA and explain to them the standing orders that were there in the LRA. Standing orders were strict rules that were to be followed by everyone in the LRA, for example, adultery was punishable by death. Anybody caught escaping would be killed. Anyone caught engaging in a sexual act with a girl who was not rightfully given to him was to be killed by the firing squad. I witnessed two couples that suffered this fate.

There was one strange rule for ladies when they were having their monthly periods. However, I dont know how women coped because there were no pads. I assume they used clean pieces of clothes. They were isolated from everyone and not touch anything that was used by the males until they were through with it. We were told that the result of their mixing up with other people who were clean was serious injuries from their opponents during fighting in the front line.

These women also had excess powers that were misused at times. They mistreated the newly abducted girls, mostly the girls who were brought to be their co-wives. This power was often through the encouragement of their bush husbands as well as from the LRA leader himself who said that no recruit should mess around with the *originals* that had for a long time suffered in the bush. The *originals* gave these girls hard work, some of which was so inhumane. A case in point was an order that was passed that saucepans be scrubbed until they shine, to the point that one would see their image as they see in a mirror. One was quoted saying, "I want to see that saucepan very clean to the point that I can see the gap in between my teeth." Others even took the newly abducted girls who were supposed to be their co-wives and thoroughly beat and strangled them in the bush just because their husband had given something new to her.

They left all the housework like washing clothes, cooking, grinding and fetching water and firewood to the newly abducted girls, while they sat, gave orders, commented negatively, and waited to eat delicious meals prepared by these very girls they were mistreating. Sometimes, the girls who prepared the food didn't even taste it. The newly abducted girls were treated as slaves, though this did not apply to all the families. In some families this mistreatment was even extended to the children born to the co-wives when their mother was not present.

As for me, I tolerated my life in Sudan from my arrival in December 1996 up to the end of 1998. At the beginning, I respected my co-wife so much, as growing up, I had been taught to respect elders. I hated using the term 'co-wives' when referring to my female friends with whom I was sharing this old man. Time and again my co-wife 'Betty' spoke ill of me in the neighbourhood, and I got to know this and kept quiet, but I blew up one day. I asked her to explain to me all the wrong things that I had ever done to her since my arrival there. She could not give me any reasonable answer. So from then on I got the courage to defend myself. Though she would still back-bite me, I took it as jealousy and went ahead with my life. I could not rival for a man I had not fallen in love with, moreover with a woman who was fit to be my mother. All I did was to make sure that I was at peace with everyone whenever and wherever possible.

To a larger extent, the commanders were to blame because they made these women big-headed by giving them power, following their tradition that a woman who was the first to be married and had stayed for a long time was to be superior over the rest. More so, these commanders acted two-sided. They provoked the originals to put pressure on the recruits so as to revenge for their earlier suffering. On the other hand, the same men told their new girls not to let the *originals* mistreat them. This ended up causing problems in the family and the originals felt that since their husbands supported them, they had the courage to go ahead and mistreat their co-wives. They controlled everything in a home such that whoever wished to access anything was to first get permission from the *original*. For example, they controlled the distribution of soap, foodstuffs and clothes, and they always did what favoured them and those they liked. Some people ended up bathing without soap, even when these first women were keeping the soap.

Although this did not happen where I stayed, my schoolmates in other positions in the same camp told me how they were being cruelly treated. One in particular told me that she was made to go several times to the other well called *kulucere* which was very far away from the LRA defense. One had to climb a very steep hill when coming out of it. On coming back, she did not even use that water but instead the jerrycan was emptied and she had to go back for more. On top of that, they were given very little food, it was not enough to survive on, and this weakened them. It was even worse when mistakes were made during cooking food. Their punishment was heavier. They would be made to eat all the food, that they didn't prepare well, for example if it was burnt. A five-litre jerrycan of water was also to be drunk by the victim under the supervision of the commanders to make them learn a lesson.

I never allowed any woman to do anything unjust while I looked on without taking a step to stop it. There was a time when we were walking to Sudan that I stopped one of my friends from carrying heavy luggage. Although an original blamed me for misleading the other schoolgirls, I felt what I did was right since my friend had an injury between her toes. I believed in speaking the truth to keep things moving on smoothly for everyone of us. Another friend of mine also told me that her co-wife always added more salt to the food she had prepared for her husband, because he always praised her for being a good cook. This act was intended to make the man hate or punish her. This happened on several occasions, but it was fortunate that the man suspected it and set a spy, who caught the woman red-handed and the evil act was ended.

Military ranks were only awarded to women who had stayed for long and persevered the suffering in the LRA.

Women who showed good leadership and hard work in a family were also given ranks under the order of Joseph Kony himself. He first investigated and consulted his top commanders before making any judgments. Then he would call everyone for a meeting where he would preach for hours about the failures, achievements and challenges, and pass orders. Ranks were given to the men who were active in the field. This system of awarding ranks was also dangerous according to my observation. It made the young men with no ranks at all and those with low ranks ambitious. They participated actively in wreaking a lot of havoc in Uganda, increasing insecurity in northern Uganda and parts of Sudan. To attain a rank, one had to be famous for committing an atrocity.

The men in the bush wanted to control women like in the old days where women had no voice. They were under the order of the army. The way women were captured and distributed made the women have no voice. Lieutenants and army officers ordered women to do things that were inhumane. For example, if a woman was called and she did not respond, she was instructed to cut thirty bundles of grass as a punishment. They gave very nasty and funny punishments using their authority. When they wanted something, you had to do it very fast like a machine. One could be sent to fetch something in the rain by a young officer. They did not mind about people's lives. What I experienced in the LRA showed me that they never valued human life. They took people's lives to be something they could mess around with whenever they felt like it.

# 7

## From schoolgirl to LRA wife

*"We acted like ladies and heroines in adversity."*

It was not easy to adjust to life in the old commander's home where I was given as a wife. I was instructed to stay only with those older women. In the beginning, there was only one wife in his home (the other was in Uganda), though he was taking care of two other women belonging to other commanders who were in Uganda. I sat quietly with them because I had nothing in common with them. All they talked about were stories related to men and how co-wives mistreat their friends. I felt very uncomfortable listening to them and had no idea that such abusive language could be uttered by women. This gave me a bad image of women in the LRA that was characterised by hatred, rumour mongering, and bad social behaviors like talking ill of others, hiding foodstuff for themselves and unnecessary glaring at those they hated plus the use of funny sign languages to hurt their friends' feelings. Those they hated were also fellow abductees, the only difference between them was the amount of time spent in the LRA.

These women had no ranks except for being an *original.* I would only answer them when I was asked anything to do with my school and how I reached Sudan. I kept on worrying about how I would get out of this life or cope with the situation since I was not used to this community where people hated their friends and spoke ill of others for no good reason. My co-wife complained about schoolgirls, saying that they are lazy, immoral and bossy. This was with an intention to hurt me, but I had no issue with her. I lived to prove to her that what she was complaining about was not true.My second co-wife, who was in Uganda when I got to Aruu, happened to be my tribemate and so friendly to me. When she came back from Uganda, my life became somehow easier since I could chat with her freely regarding things from home.

From my experience in the LRA, those who were literate and spoke English were the most hated by the majority of the population that did not get the chance to either go to school or complete their studies. And whenever we spoke, especially in English, they accused us of making plans to get our freedom and so we were reported to the top commanders. Those found guilty received penalties like death, segregation or severe punishments.  Because the others did not either understand or speak English or both, they were always suspicious of those of us who knew it well. If someone in the LRA knew you had gone to school, they considered you a proud person and criticised you, most especially the women and some commanders who did not get the chance to study before they were abducted.

We were segregated from the others because of this. The group of girls abducted from my school suffered most from this segregation because Joseph Kony himself openly spoke of things that annoyed the LRA women even before our arrival. In a vision, he said the girls he was to bring would be educated (meaning the Aboke girls), and those who did not go to school would be the ones to wash their feet, among other comments that angered the uneducated women. By the time we arrived at the LRA base in Sudan, the women already had negative feelings about us, and they planned evil ways to mistreat us. My limited formal education was not of any advantage to me while in captivity. In any case, it caused me more pain. For instance, my co-wives always glared at me whenever I spoke or interpreted any piece of information in English. Nasty comments were made and this made life hard for me as I felt so downhearted.

One time I came across four of my friends who were my schoolmates. This was in Nicitu which was one of the many places that the LRA lived. In English we discussed how each one's life was going and then tried to encourage each other to be strong as there was no other way out of the LRA. This was misinterpreted as a plan to escape yet we were just excited to see each other after a long time and have that precious moment to discuss our issues. After this, one of my friends escaped two days later because she was being mistreated by some of her co-wives. This happened in Joseph Kony's home, and his chief security guard mainly blamed me for her escape, saying that of all the schoolgirls, I was the one who knew all the secrets among the Aboke girls. I was to be punished if she was not found but they found her. As a result of this, an order was given by Joseph Kony that any schoolgirls within the LRA camp found talking to each other should be shot instantly. For us who had been abducted from Aboke, it was stressful because we were always being watched.

To live peacefully among the LRA required the following from a girl: She was to be a good cook, obedient, well-behaved, a clean person, tolerant, calm, flexible and hard-working. Without those qualities, the results were problematic. Even with all that, a girl still had problems as a result of hatred and jealousy among co-wives, that at times went beyond limits.

I did all that was expected of a good woman to avoid problems, though I still encountered negative responses from my co-wives, especially the oldest one. Despite all I did, she would still back-bite me to her friends, saying that I was loved more than any other woman. I lost my respect for her because she took advantage of my silence to abuse me without any cause, which I later learnt was jealousy. She didn't hold any military ranks, but I respected her since she was the first woman there. She was the one to measure out foodstuffs. She was also the one to serve certain kinds of dishes when cooked, but from my observation, she was not doing it well. She was dishonest, greedy and selfish. When meat was cooked (it was scarce), she ate a bigger share, leaving us with lots of soup and very few pieces.

At times, she reduced grains that were to be ground into flour, this meant that the size of bread to be mingled would be small and insufficient for all. This caused complaints from the boys and resulted in a change in command to me. I took control of the store and things changed for the better. Boys were no longer complaining, she tried all she could to take this position away from me. For example, she accused me of stealing goat's meat and other false accusations like wasting food. She always said that I had been given power to control the food store because I went to school and was favoured. I saw no reason why I should be jealous for a man I had not chosen for myself. After all, we were all abductees. So I found it useless to behave the way she was doing and I continued to live a normal life with my co-wives. Whenever an issue arose, we solved it diplomatically and openly.

An incident also occurred whereby one time some boys went for an operation and brought with them a goat's thigh that was to be smoked and prepared for the mess (a high table that comprised of commanders with similar ranks who gathered to eat at their superior's place). Food from their particular homes was gathered in that one place so as it would be shared by all their wives. So we left this meat, the goat's thigh, on the fire in the kitchen to smoke and went for supper. By then, we were preparing meals for about seven boys and five girls. We called one of the boys to come and pick their food and instead, he called his friends and they cut part of the meat. Unfortunately, when the girl removed this meat from the fire and took it to my hut, she did not check it before taking it.

The next morning, I got up very early and went up to Joseph Kony's place where I was to help in cooking as there was a function that involved all the highly-ranked people. I did not know that something had happened to the piece of meat that was taken to my hut. When I came back in the evening, I found my older co-wife seated under a tree but when she saw me, she frowned as she normally did, and I realised there was something wrong. I asked another girl who told me about the issue of the meat, that my co-wife was saying I was the one who had cut the meat. So I confronted her and our commander got to know about it. Then, he called all of us and asked what the problem was. My co-wife accused me of theft but I had no record of theft during my stay there.

After two weeks, when I was already in another defense called Bin Rwot, the real thieves were discovered. One boy was caught in the act during another incident where the thieves stole *sim-sim* and the small green peas, *coroko*. Some of the boys and girls he had conspired with had prepared the food and refused to give it to him, so he decided to remove a portion of the bread from their meal and hid it in his trousers. It later fell out in front of his friend. This annoyed the friends and they made fun of him, he also became angry and revealed all the secrets about their theft. This openly proved that my co-wife's accusation was untrue. This is the kind of hatred and jealousy that the abducted girls went through within the LRA.

I think women acted that way because of jealousy as many women were competing for one man's favour. Again, most women were abducted from villages where they saw how village women behaved with their co-wives. To add on to that, women wanted to have an easy life at the expense of whoever they could take advantage of, especially the newly abducted.

As school girls, generally we encountered difficulties of various types, most especially with the female originals. This was mainly because we could speak English and had attained education at least up to the secondary level compared to the majority of young ladies we found in the LRA. To them, speaking English was the secret to a man's heart, as most of the men in the LRA prioritised school girls. So the originals looked at school girls that had been integrated among the rebels as a threat to their bush marriages.

More so, school girls usually showed good behavior like obedience and tolerance with no thoughts of revenge on those who mistreated them, and the rebel commanders who tried to get the *originals* to change their arrogant ways used us as examples. This caused more hatred towards. Whenever we spoke, they suspected that we were back-biting them or planning to escape. For this we faced segregation in whichever positions we were distributed. The hatred was in the form of obscene language, being given little food, and difficult manual work. In my case, sometimes when I was listening to the BBC news, we were all seated by a fireplace in the evenings, a mere interpretation of the news headlines called for a bad comment from my first co-wife, which was intended to hurt my feelings. One day I made cassava chips by deep frying a few slices of cassava. This caused hatred from one of the women I was living with in the same position.

All this was an attempt to demoralise us so that our level was reduced to theirs. Since we had nowhere to turn to, we patiently persevered through all forms of torture that we were put through. We acted like ladies and heroines in adversity. No matter what was said or done, we always had hope that one day we would be free by the grace of God.

When I had just arrived in Sudan, John told me, "Not everything you hear in this place from people is right. You always have to make your own judgments. Others will bring you gossip so that you fall in trouble, so you have got to be careful." At first I used to respect Betty, the senior wife, as my elder but a time came when she would attack me openly saying, "Students do not know how to work, not even sweeping. Why don't you plant your own okra other than eating the ones that I have planted?" One time I confronted her and we quarreled. From then on she realised I could also stand my ground at times and she began to fear me. After that, I only respected her for what was necessary but whenever she would do anything that was related to both physical and mental torture, I would not keep quiet but react to defend myself. Despite all that happened to me, I took it easy because I realised that as long as I was alive, bush life would not be my final destination.

In late January 1999, I realised I was pregnant. At the camp it was very easy to tell when a woman was pregnant since she took long to isolate herself and also the signs like morning sickness would start being noticed. I did not get any special attention or treatment from John just because I was pregnant, all he would be thinking about were security matters. Despite all the hardships on 30th of September, I gave birth to my first child. I didn't know anything about having a baby. There was no hospital in the base or trained midwives. At one point I was allowed to go to Juba for antenatal care at the hospital, however, I was closely guarded and not allowed to speak to anyone because they were afraid that someone would discover I was one of the Aboke girls and help me plan my escape. When my labour pains started, one of the elderly women who helped others give birth, also helped me. It took so long, and I kept thinking of another young girl who died in hospital after it was discovered she needed a c-section. So I was so afraid of undergoing a c-section. After a long time, they took me to the Juba hospital. It was raining, and there was only me and the elderly woman and I gave birth immediately, it did not take long. When they left me, I was alone with the baby. I had no idea what to do, how to clean or care for the baby. No one was there at all. I remember I was very hungry and I asked someone to bring me some food. What they brought was not edible. Eventually a commander came to see me, and he was angry I had even interacted with that person to find food for me. I was taken back to John's house in an adjacent LRA defense next to Juba called Nicitu.

# 8

# The man in the bush

*"He was the most quarrelsome being I have ever met on this planet."*

When my first born, Ogen was around six months old, we shifted from Nicitu II to a new base called Rubangatek, established as a safe place away from the front line and the Arabs. The water source was the Kit River. Before we left, Arabs had given the LRA foodstuffs. For example, in our home we had four sacks of sugar of about 100 kilograms each. Each commander was given one hundred kilograms. One good thing about this man I lived with was that he was not strict over food. He would say, "You eat but do not waste." He told us to economise the food and prepare what was enough for everyone. Then, all foodstuffs were taken to Rubangatek, the new place. There was no house yet so the sacks were kept outside. We would pick like ten cups and then sew up the sack. We came for more if it got finished. One day, a boy used my needle to sew up the sack of sugar. He then put the needle in the mattress and it got lost. When I asked him, he could not find it. Then after a while, the man in the bush sent for the mattress and found the needle in it. When I went there he asked me, "Whose needle is this?" I told him it was mine and I explained to him how it got there because I recognised it from the colour of thread used. He took it that I had placed that needle there intentionally to bewitch him as he had recently taken up another young girl to be his wife. In other words, he was saying that I was practicing witchcraft on him.

Funny enough, out of his relatives who used to visit him, one of them was a witch. She explained after she was caught in the act that she used a needle to bewitch men so that they fail to become erect when they were with other women apart from her. She said she also put a safety pin on her private parts for the same purpose. It was not my first time to hear witchcraft cases among his relatives. There were also other relatives of his who were witches. One of them was our neighbour then and the other was married to another man, so all these gave me a clear idea that there was an element of witchcraft at the home of my bush husband in Uganda.

One day, I had gone to get local salt (*kado atwona*) from one of the defenses where my bush husband was then living. He watched me but I did not mind him. I kept on gathering the stems of the herb which I was going to burn for the local salt. In the evening he called us together. He began to talk about the needle issue. The new wife he had brought was about thirteen years old. They used to turn girls into wives as soon as they began to menstruate. This was how the men in the bush judged if a girl was mature enough to be a wife.

I became furious and confronted him because he was accusing me of being a witch. When I get angry, I have the courage to utter anything. We were not staying far from Kony's place. I told him, "How can you consider me to be a witch and yet you have no proof. I have evidence about your family being witches. Let me not hear you call me a slut or a witch again!" I raised my voice in anger. He got scared and my co-wives too were scared. Bodyguards from Kony's home were sent to find out what the matter was. I do not know what explanation he gave them anyway.

One day he reminded me of the incident and said, "You Langi are big-headed, too frank, and you say things in the open." I told him, "I do not back-bite anyone. I always tell the truth in the open." I was free and could speak out my mind. John taught us that it is the devil that makes people keep secrets, so we had to speak out whatever bothered us. He would not judge us based on gossip. The good thing about my bush husband was that he solved issues fairly. He called everyone together and listened to both parties including witnesses before he judged at a family level. According to the African culture, a father in a family is the final man in resolving family issues, unless the case at hand is too much for him to handle then he can take it to his clan members. One time Betty lied about me, but she was proved wrong after my witnesses spoke.

Over time, I got to know the reason why Betty hated me. According to her old stories, she would lamented about being childless, since her first marriage from home in 1980. I could tell she was desperate for a child as she explained her problem regarding this to Joseph Kony, who had prescribed for her various local herbs to take but they failed. She had given up on the issue of bearing children. Her comment when I gave birth to my first child showed me that she was not happy.

It was at the same time John, our bush husband, had just picked the young girl for a wife. Betty said to her friend who had come to see my baby, "You see, now he has taken another woman who will bear him another bouncing baby boy. Do you think he can even dream about some of us?" In our culture it is such an offence to say such a comment. It was not a surprise to me when she later chased my baby-sitter who was carrying my baby from where she was supposed to hide from a helicopter gunship that resulted in the loss of their lives. Though she played with the child, she was not so happy. If someone saw her from a distance carrying the baby, they would not know the grudge she had. She used to talk ill of me to her friends because of this child. She also ate all the food that was meant for the children when we were back in Uganda in 2004, and left a small portion that was not enough for them. She complained that I took a bigger potion because I had a child. At times, she was good but it would not last long.

The man in the bush is so far the most quarrelsome being I have ever met on this planet. He was always suspicious, blamed and punished anybody at any time without a proper reason, and everyone in the LRA wondered how some of us who were staying in the same compound with him managed. We developed survival strategies, like keeping quiet and continuing with our businesses, avoiding the use of words that were linked to old age like grey hair, and so on. I got fed up with quarrels and arguments, and up to now, I do not stay where arguments are going on to create a peaceful environment for myself.

One day I was chatting with Betty, John sat as he used to, facing us, and watching our movements all the time. If one was afraid of being watched, he or she would not have the courage to move because of his scary eyes. He called us one evening and began to quarrel. He said, "You women are always jealous. Now you are competing before me to impress me so that I call both of you to sleep with me today." I asked him, "Are you not sick in the head? We are not competing. We are discussing our own business." He uttered very bad words concerning prostitution, and I kept quiet. He thought that students were taught about sex education in schools and so they all practiced it. He asked me several times whether we were given sex education. One day he asked me, "Were you taught sex education?" I answered him. "I was abducted when I did not know anything about sex. I was not a slut and there is no way I could practice the act just from the blue, so do not grade me in the group of prostitutes." He kept quiet as he always did when told facts.

One day when we were in Rubangatek, I sneezed around 10 am. That mere act of sneezing aloud made him angry with me. He said, "Is that a new way of sneezing?" I first laughed because it was funny and said, "Is sneezing not allowed in this place?" He was ashamed because that act of sneezing was not genuine enough for his rude comment.

One day during Christmas in 2003 when almost all the LRA was in Uganda and other minority were dancing at night and making merriments, John shouted extremely aloud to alert the whole defence "You are messing with your husbands' escorts in the absence of your husbands and you are enjoying yourselves, but time will come when you will pay for it all." He used to shout a lot with no good reason. This was seasonal. At times when he was feeling sick, he thought that people were the ones making him sick. He asked the escorts what they were up to and things they did not know. When not in a good mood, he used to ask very funny questions that showed he was suspicious.

John used to quarrel a lot when there were rumours of attack threatening our security. He acted as though we were the ones who caused the problems. He quarreled over small issues. One day, when we were back in Uganda in 2004, I was correcting my son, but he took it for mistreatment and told me that I should leave his son alone. He went on to say that I should escape and go to my husbands, the UPDF, if I wanted, but leave him alone with his son.

I didn't like being blamed for what I had not done. I would confront him after he had quarreled. I always told him facts. He said I did not like his son. He told me he would kill me if his son died. I asked him, "How can I neglect my own son?" When we sat together as women, he always confronted us by asking us what we were up to. He said that he had studied psychology and he knew how women think. He would ask us, *"Ikin an ki wun, anga ma okwongo neno olwit?"* (Between you and me, who was the first to see a hawk period?). By this he would be asking who was the first to be born, as he was ever suspicious that people talked about his age and grey hair. Of course he was older than all of us, but he felt embarrassed that he was staying with ladies who were much younger. He always told us that he was more experienced than us and also complained that we always made fun of him because he was old, as if we would not grow old.

# 9

# On the run in Sudan

*"We started living like the real gorillas in the bush."*

When we first arrived in Sudan, we were told to forget about Uganda. I thought I would die in Sudan. I had no hope of one day coming back to Uganda. Other people, including some of my schoolmates, would take tins containing bullets to the border of Uganda from Sudan. I was not allowed to go anywhere other than stay in the defenses that we transferred to year after year until we moved from Sudan during "Operation Iron Fist" in 2002.

## Jebelen

Combined forces of Ugandan soldiers and the SPLA attacked us in April 1997, driving us out of Aruu. After the battle in Aruu, we went to Jebelen I and two brigades were taken to Jebelen II, where the cases of witchcraft took place.

On arrival in Jebelen I, we settled along Juba Road on a plain. The department that I belonged to was called Chief defense, and as members of that department, we were directed to stay where there was a big tree for a position. At first, the place seemed scary because the combined forces of Sudanese soldiers and the Ugandan government were still pursuing the LRA rebels even after taking over the defense of Aruu. Most of the time, the LRA were ready to take off. Then, I was not allowed to move alone when going to fetch water at a nearby river or searching for wild plants for food.

One day, we picked the wildest species of plant that looked edible, but we failed to eat it due to its bitterness. We threw it away and took porridge that day though we were hungry. It so happened that one morning, as a group of thirty soldiers were making their usual routine of patrolling round the defense, they came across their opponents, the UPDF, who had just reached the defense and were digging *adakis* and planning to attack both the LRA and the Arabs in the Sudanese Army. This was in Jebelen I.

The news about this reached Jebelen defence at around 9 am using a walkie-talkie and instantly the field commander sounded a very loud whistle to alert everyone to run to the frontline. I could not imagine myself in the frontline with all the fear that I was holding within me. The active soldiers were willingly running to face the combined forces of Sudanese rebels and the Ugandan soldiers, cocking their guns and shouting in excitement as they refilled their magazines with bullets to go 'charging,' looting new uniforms from their enemies after killing them. For me who was a coward and ignorant in the battlefield, I decided to remain and wait to run for my dear life when the LRA rebels were defeated. So I gathered my few belongings that I was given by those who frequently went on operations in Uganda, and got set for the run. In just less than thirty minutes, the sound of all sorts of guns began rocking the air for over three hours. It sounded like the roofs of houses with iron sheets were being hit or banged using sticks. Those of us who did not go to the frontline, we were on the go or on standby.

As for me, I was only waiting to hear bullets directed towards the Jebelen defence, then I would take off to Juba for safety. But it so happened that the LRA rebels overpowered their opponents and drove them out of the area because items like medicine, new uniforms, foodstuffs, guns and pouches for holding magazines were being brought including two dead bodies. One soldier belonging to the Ugandan government was captured.

Later in the evening that day, people went to see the bodies of the two dead men as the one who was alive was being seriously interrogated by Lt. Col. Otti Vincent, who was in charge of the operation room. When I was told about this, I got scared of seeing dead bodies. More so, I remembered the sight of those who had been wounded by the bullet on our walk to Sudan, and the horrible sight of blood oozing from their wound. However, I gathered my courage and proceeded to see the dead men. Some people were joking that the recruits should go see the dead people to make sure the dead that were not their relatives. The dead men lay, naked except for their underpants, facing the sky with their eyes closed as though they were merely sleeping, without any sign of the bullet having pierced their bodies. They looked so normal and clean as though their bodies were cleaned, the sight was not as scarely as I thought.

Standing before Vincent Otti was the other soldier who had been caught alive from the frontline. He was looking so confused, surprised and scared, as his big eyes kept on rolling all round seeing the huge number of rebel soldiers coming to see him and his dead colleagues. Seeing him in that state made me imagine what he was thinking and what his fate would be and I sympathised and prayed to God for his dear life, which was at threat. He was later handed over to the Sudanese government.

To the LRA, this was good luck as their victory in the frontline pleased the Sudanese government as well. A lot of food was donated to the LRA at the end of every month. This included cooking oil, sugar, wheat flour, beans, tea leaves, and cow peas, among others that are in Sudanese terms like *tania* (this was a Sudanese snack made from sesame/sim-sim and sugar). Since then, life changed positively as food was enough, and for about five months, there was no attack from the Ugandan government. Even the lives of the lowliest group of people improved and the death rate declined except for the shortage of water. We were fetching water from a seasonal river that was a tributary of Kit River. This river would collect all the dirty materials from upland to the river and later it was fetched for domestic use even if it was reddish brown in color because it was the only source of water.

When the rain took long to fall, shortage of water would be experienced so we had to move along the river valley in search of water. One time we came into contact with some of the inhabitants who lived along that river, and at first they were scared of LRA rebels because all the time they were armed with guns. Later, they got used to us and established a strong relationship where transactions developed in the form of barter trade. This relationship eventually broke down because some of the LRA soldiers went to loot from these people and killed others.

## Nicitu

From Jebelen II, we went to Nicitu in 1998. Nicitu existed even when LRA was still in Aruu. This was the safest place for mothers and those who were wounded and became permanently disabled. It was a safe place near Juba town. The electricity lights could even be seen. But whenever I saw the light, I was always reminded of home in Uganda where I would have been in a well lit house. Instead, I was living a life that was full of uncertainties.

When we arrived in Sudan, the Ugandan government kept sending their troops annually. The LRA decided to take mothers to Nicitu because it was safe there. When the relationship between the LRA, Arabs and the Sudanese was broken, I went to Nicitu II. It was an extended inland for safety, as there was a misunderstanding between the Sudanese government and the LRA rebels. They all decided to lead separate lives.

Big grass thatched houses were built here, but only Betty and I had the task of cutting grass that was to be used for building one big hut. Every morning we cut *akida* (a type of grass used for building huts) using sickles. We piled it in big bundles. That was our duty for two solid months. What I discovered with the LRA commanders was that they aimed at keeping everyone busy by creating work. For example, almost every year from 1998 we were cutting grass for roofing in new establishments until the year 2000.

Rubangatek, Bin Rwot, and Odek were places where the LRA lived. Odek was the southwest from Bin Rwot. Huts were built deep in the jungle where nobody except the LRA members knew their location and people were distributed for safety since Joseph Kony saw it as a risk to put all of us together in case of an attack. Had we continued to move, we would have reached the Ugandan border from Bin Rwot. We could hear sounds of vehicles from an area that connected Sudan to Uganda called Cindru.

Bin Rwot came up as a result of the breakup of the relationship between the Arabs and the LRA. They said it is the Lord who should come and help them. Bin Rwot means, "Come Oh Lord." The LRA members said they did not know what to do, whether to mend the relationship or do anything else that would be good for them. After Bin Rwot, Kony told people to name their homes according to the name of their villages in Uganda. This was after establishing another place for settlement of which his was Odek, as his home in Uganda is in Odek. For example, if someone came from Pabbo, he would name it Pabbo.

## Operation Iron Fist-Lalar, 2002

There was another place called Lalar, which means 'saviour'. It was near a rock. This is where the Iron Fist operation took place. By the time we left Lalar, we had grown plenty of food crops that would have lasted for about three years without anybody complaining of hunger. In my home, we had a very big heap of sorghum grains, eight sacks of tiny green peas (*lugwiri*) of about one hundred kilograms each, six sacks of *sim-sim*, four sacks of pigeon peas (*lapena*) and millet. To any original in the LRA, this was a lot of food and it implied that people were not going to suffer from hunger. Others even reared chicken. We lived like we were at home in a Ugandan village in an African traditional setting where a family had a homestead with a very large courtyard. All in all, the LRA aimed at making wherever they settled a nice place to live in even if they were only going to live there for a short period. Although they would burn other people's houses, they made sure what belonged to them was safe-guarded. However, after the Iron Fist Operation that started in February 2002, life became challenging for all the members of LRA rebels who were not used to mobile life.

In an attempt to secure some of my belongings like clothes, cooking utensils and some of the foodstuffs that my family members and I managed to sneak away from the UPDF soldiers, boys dug deep holes and hid the items with the hope of finding them later after the war. But we were deceiving ourselves, as we did not find a thing after the thorough operation done by the UPDF. They either burnt or carried away the remaining portion of the foodstuffs from the LRA camps.

Four days after the first attack of Operation Iron Fist, we started living like the real gorillas in the bush. Since there were more ladies with children than men in the LRA, the whole area where we camped was full of noise from babies crying. They were not used to the new life in the jungle. I got a lot of difficulties starting the long journey that was to end in the Imatong ranges, in the southeastern part of southern Sudan.

That afternoon was a very hot one, and the heavy weight I was carrying on my head plus my two-year-old baby on my back were such a burden. My heart doubled its normal beat when I heard those in the operation room whistling to alert everyone that it was time to get on the move. I carried my baby on my back, then I was helped to lift my luggage on my head and off I went, though the weight I was carrying on my head was too heavy for me to move for long distances. I kept stopping time and again to rest. It was late in the night when the long line of people, came to a halt and positions were distributed for the night for people to sleep.

With my chest aching due to the heavy weight I carried, I made a temporary bed out of dry grass under a tree and spent my night. But it was the same story the next day as the whistling came even earlier. We carried on with the journey until midday when we stopped to prepare lunch by a riverside and slept there as we had no hope of getting another source of water. Having been tortured by the heavy load, all I thought of was reducing the load on my head, so I reduced the 15 kilograms of peas by two kilos, by cooking it for that day's meal, but still suffered with the weight of 20 pieces of soap plus my few clothes as I could not do without them.

That evening, we could hear from our positions many vehicles that were transporting the UPDF and their tanks into Sudan, this was very terrifying. The sound came from all directions so I thought we might come across the UPDF as we crossed the famous Aruu Road, but we crossed safely the following night. I associated the sound from the tanks with the dangerous bombs that they dropped as I had witnessed from the Aruu attack in 1997, which I survived without any injuries. I had a sleepless night thinking of how the huge convoy of LRA that consisted of only a few fighters would survive in case the ambitious UPDF soldiers found us.

# 10

## Flight to the Imatong Mountains

*"Nearly the whole village was massacred."*

It took us about three weeks to reach the Imatong mountains. This was our first long movement after five good years. We carried our babies on our backs and sometimes had to move in the rain and at times even at night. We climbed the many hills with much difficulty. We were excited that we were going to live in a place where there was plenty of food, since ours had been burnt down by the UPDF.

The first place we entered was Tebika. Tebika was cold, hilly and forested. There are huge trees with parasitic plants growing on their trunks. There were banana plantations on gently sloping hills that the convoy cut for food. In between the hills were broad, deep valleys with rivers that flowed with ice cold water. To me, life in this new place was a burden because of the cold weather, steep hills, constant rain and the tiresome, endless movement across steep hills and forest. It was really so difficult for me to adjust life here.

We had to move every day in order to keep a distance between us and the UPDF who were pursuing us. Some people would sleep along the way before reaching the next position. This is because they were overloaded with foodstuffs, beddings, clothing and cooking utensils, in addition to babies on their backs. Those who had more than one child could only carry one, so the other children, some as young as three, would have to walk. I had a two-year-old boy who was ever on my back all the time, I felt he was too young to walk long distances like the adults. I chose to bear the burden of his weight rather than make him suffer the way I saw other children of his age being harassed to climb the steep hills fast. Others would fall down due to the slippery paths. The older boys who were assigned to carry them would mistreat them. It was worse when it rained, for the kids shivered from the cold yet nobody was bothered about their condition.

Sometimes when I was moving, I saw other people on the next hill, looking so tiny like little insects slowly moving uphill. I wondered then whether I would reach there. But a step at a time, I also reached the position after resting several times on the way. In the cold weather, I saw people sweating when climbing the hills. The next village that we passed through was Pucoka. In this village, the LRA were still disciplined and the inhabitants of this village were friendly because they also spoke Acholi, a common language that was spoken among the LRA. The two parties even did barter trade. LRA rebels offered clothes in exchange for foodstuffs like *matooke* (plantains), beans, potatoes, pumpkins and others. However, some young boys would sneak and steal foodstuffs belonging to these inhabitants. This act broke the relationship between the LRA and the people of Pucoka, which resulted in an abrupt evacuation of the LRA from their land when the UPDF moved closer to the LRA camp.

I remember the first night we had in Pucoka. Joseph Kony told us that the next day we would leave for another place, but we did not because my co-wife went into labour. After she delivered, the next day the whole convoy set off for another place called Katire that was still safe. I will never forget that day's journey. Having rained heavily the previous night, we set off to climb a very high mountain directly without creating a winding path to dodge the steep hills. This time, I tried my best to reach the next position in time since we were informed that the UPDF soldiers were not far from us and some were running away from them. One step at a time, I kept going up the hill while supporting myself with trees and resting against them whenever I got tired. It was with a lot of difficulty that I made it after about five hours.

I reached that night's position late in the evening and it soon started to rain. I untied my little boy from my back and went to look for firewood, water and somewhere to grind millet for some porridge which would be our supper. That evening, it rained before I finished grinding so I carried the little flour I had ground and picked my small mobile grinding stone and rushed down the hill to my position. My position was very cold as it was located under big tall trees whose leaves had for a long time been rotting.

When it started raining, all I thought of was my co-wife and her one-day-old baby in the chilly evening without even a mere tent to shelter them from the rain. I never figured out how she managed to climb the steep, slippery hill with all her hands holding the newborn baby on her belly. At last she reached safely and got shelter in our mobile tent that was carried by the boys.

Due to the nature of the landscape, very many people slept along the way in the chilly, damp forest, and the following morning they proceeded to the next position. One can only imagine how babies and pregnant women managed to survive in the harsh, chilly, conditions during this period without falling sick. This reminds me of what Joseph Kony told the LRA rebels before the Operation Iron Fist attack. "We shall win this war by moving away from the enemy because if we are to fight, then we are going to lose all these women who are non-fighters. So when we tell you to move, do so, because that is one of the ways we shall be defeating the Ugandan government troops." This message encouraged the LRA members who were too weak to move whenever they were ordered to. Even those who had only one leg had to limp in order to dodge the Ugandan army.

We arrived in Katire, a place that is located in a flat land surrounded by ranges of mountains, the highest of which is Imatong Mountain. This is where nearly the whole village was massacred, to clear way for our passage. This order came after LRA soldiers realised that these villagers had participated in fighting against them when they were crossing Magui Road, one of the main roads that ran from Uganda to Sudan. Normally, the order of our movement would be as follows: first, the stand-by that comprised of well-armed soldiers ready for any attack. They would then clear the way so that the non-fighters could move and stay in a safe place.

At that time we had no food, so we were feeding on the bean leaves that we had carried from Rubangatek which got finished. There was a lot of food in Katire and it was the kind of place we were all eager to get so we could settle and eat. To us food was so important yet so scarce.

However, before we left for Katire, I saw new people being brought in to the LRA camp. We were told that they were the inhabitants of Katire village. One of the boys in that stand-by who was staying in my position (home) narrated to me that Nyeko Tolbert Yadin, who was the head of operation, had gone to Katire and found the villagers gathered for a burial. When he asked a the cause of death, he was told that the army commander died in a fight between the LRA and the Sudanese soldiers in Magui Road. These villages spoke oblivious to the fact that they were talking to LRA rebels dressed in army uniform.

So Yadin called Joseph Kony and he was instructed to wipe out the whole village. Consequently, Yadin used his tricks to convince the Katire men to surrender their guns and the whole village was arrested. Men, women, and children alike. Men were tied and marched uphill to the LRA position with their women and children. Joseph Kony himself called everyone and said, "From today on, do not look at anyone outside the LRA as a friend because all these Sudanese inhabitants have guns and are against the LRA rebels. So kill whoever you come across." The Katire women and children were already being starved in the LRA camp.

I remember that morning after coming back from where Joseph Kony was addressing us I saw children of less than three years crying aloud while looking into their mothers' eyes because of hunger. I felt so sorry for them and yet I could do nothing to help. They were being punished for something they had no idea about. Meanwhile, their fathers were being pushed in the deep valleys with their hands tied up. A boy in the LRA who had gone down to Katire to get foodstuffs came and told us jokingly that he was tired of killing the men in Katire. And indeed he looked so because his shirt had sprinkles of blood on it. The rebels used the Katire men to ferry all the foodstuffs that belonged to the them like groundnuts, *sim-sim*, beans and sorghum. These men were later killed after reaching the LRA camp. Later in the afternoon, non-fighters were told to move to a safer place ahead on the next hill as UPDF were getting closer to where we were. We left the Katire women and children in the ditch with their fate unknown to us.

From then, our main work was to move as much as we could in order to keep a distance between us and the UPDF. It took me about six hours to reach the new position at the hill top using a path that was being slashed for us. I got so tired of climbing up the hill with the baby on my back that I kept on resting along the path after every ten minutes. We passed through thick undergrowth of tall, densely-populated, wild trees and made our way to a place we thought was safer, higher in altitude and hidden. Little did we know that the UPDF soldiers were taking the shortest possible route to reach us.

After just two nights, a boy on observation post (OP) brought a message that the UPDF soldiers were coming towards us. Later, in the afternoon we carried our few belongings and went very fast down the hill to Katire, as they had already started shelling (throwing bombs from a distance). We were warned not to take any water on the way, as it was contaminated by the dead bodies of the people of Katire. Indeed the stench from the nearby bushes as we went downhill was unbearable. If you were not strong enough you would vomit.

Within me, there was no peace. I kept on thinking about the people of Katire, how they had perished, and of their vacant flat land surrounded by ranges of hills. I imagined how peaceful they were in this fertile land, but in just a matter of days they were no more. This was a violation of human rights but I had no voice as I was then a victim of these inhumane acts of the LRA. My point of view was that one must be punished for what he or she has done, but many should not be made to suffer because a few are guilty.

In order for us to rest, about one hundred experienced LRA soldiers were chosen to go and face the UPDF soldiers under Joseph Kony's orders. He foretold their victory. Consequently, the following morning we were on our marks on hearing several gunshots including bombs. This occurred as early as 6 am, but we were assured of our safety, it was an ambush set by the LRA soldiers. After hearing that we at last rested from the UPDF attacks.

We hurriedly crossed from Katire to the other slope of the hill hoping to find a place to rest for some days on one of the high Imatong mountain ranges, and evade the Ugandan troops. There we lived in isolated hills for safety and food was obtained from the Sudanese inhabitants, who grew maize, potatoes, beans and other vegetables like cabbage and pumpkins.

Life on these hills became extremely hard because of the cold weather which I was not used to, coupled with constant rainfall. And with the poor shelter we had, life was not easy. The rain clouds that I used to see very high in the sky when I was on a flat land were then very close, and I could see them passing over my head and among the tree branches. They moved with a cold wind that made the weather so chilly. Whenever I saw the sun shining brightly on the flat ground far away from us, I wished I was there to enjoy the warm sunshine rather than sitting by the fireplace all day long warming myself. Indeed, just like some musician said "you will only need the sun when it starts to snow."

*Apwap* (a name given by LRA to one of the Imatong ranges, was situated at the border of Sudan and Uganda. It was a no man's land but the LRA paved our way for safety and we settled there for at least two months. This name Apwap, (coined by Joseph Kony) came from the way it was hidden among the hills. It was discovered by the stand-bys as a suitable position where we could stay in October. Everyone in the group liked it here because of the location and the landscape. The range had about four flat topped hills, each separated by a slow flowing stream. The vegetation was composed of short grass and a few tall trees with green parasitic plants growing on their trunks. These were located only at the tops of the hills. Between each hill was short grass that made the scenery so beautiful when viewed from the top of the hills. One could watch the other move from one hill to another perfectly well. The only problem was with the weather. It was an extremely cold place with a lot of rainfall received at any moment. I had never been to such a place where the Nimbus clouds that brought rain could pass over the tree just above my head in the form of mist. As a result, we spent most of the time by the fireplace warming ourselves in the small grass thatched kitchen that we made. Worst of all, the water was ice-cold. For one to bathe the sun had to be shining and the water had to be warm like at around 1 pm.

At least firewood was in abundance. We cut it from dry wood and split them into small pieces using an axe, and used the pieces for cooking and warming ourselves.

What I hated most in Apwap was cutting grass for roofing, digging and hunger. We had to cut grass for roofing three huts. However, the species of grass there was very short and situated at the foot of the hills. Every day we had to cut about four bundles and carry them all uphill. Not only that, food here was also completely scarce. A few able boys and girls were selected to go where the Sudanese people were living to loot food from their gardens after fighting them. The only food that would last and available in abundance was maize. So we roasted and ate it in form of hard corns or roasted and ground it to make a little porridge to which we added salt to make sauce. We then mingled posho (corn bread) from the remaining maize flour. That was what we fed on in Apwap for the more than two months that we lived there. If we found beans, we also roasted and ground them to sauce from the flour. This was to make it last longer as we were many in our family.

As a result of inadequate food, Joseph Kony gave an order that people should begin farming since the place was peaceful and the land was fertile. Thereafter, we tilled the land surrounding our home and planted maize and beans. This was not an easy thing for me. It involved clearing the grass, removing it from the garden and then planting. The soil was too heavy to lift with a hoe because of the heavy rainfall, and I did not have enough energy because of the kind of food we ate. However, many boys heaped Joseph Kony's potatoes to over ten thousand heaps. For about a month, these boys did not miss a single day of heaping potatoes.

Generally life was not easy for me so what I did to keep busy was making clothes. I did that for free for whoever brought her pieces to me from the little knowledge I had. I made a sweater for my son out of my school sweater after realising how cold Apwap was. One time, we ran short of food and a stand-by was prepared to go to a place called Agoro for food. Two boys escaped but one unfortunately was caught. The other managed to get away. The former was killed and the boys from the stand-by brought his red pair of trousers to prove they had actually killed him. The other one who escaped returned with the UPDF soldiers to attack us in Apwap.

## Attack in Apwap

It happened that Kony was preparing to go down to the flat land where we had lived before being attacked by the UPDF in the Iron Fist operation (near Juba). The main purpose of his going was to renew their relationship with the Sudanese government since the Ugandan soldiers had already left there. We were attacked that morning when he left. When he was leaving, I remember him telling John that he should be careful and put security on the route that the stand-bys who went to Agoro used. Unknown to us, the UPDF soldiers had then lined up to the East and were more than ready to attack us. Some people saw them lining up but did not think they were dangerous people. Others said they thought those were stand-bys arriving from outside as that was the time when Joseph Kony and his guards left. No sooner had Kony left than they began shooting.

Then, my son had asked me to let him go and play with the boys at the *adaki* side. But I refused because it was too early for him to leave. He insisted but I told him that he would miss my sweets and he was convinced to come with me to the kitchen where I was both warming myself and making people's dresses. The attack started with a bomb early in the morning at around 7.30 am. On hearing it, I got up at once and held my baby's hand. I ran as fast as I could to the next hut to pick my bed sheet so I could tie my baby on my back. By this time several small machine guns were being fired all over the place and it was mostly concentrating on the hill where Kony and John were, as they were among the top commanders. From the way the bullets were being aimed, I think the UPDF had been briefed on which positions belonged to those commanders. Most bombs dropped on the hill where Joseph Kony and John were located.

As soon as I left the hut, a bomb fell on it and it was burnt. I rushed down the slope looking for a safer zone. I was nearly hit by a bomb, which passed over my head and hit a nearby bush. Fortunately, I was going downhill; otherwise, it would have slashed my head off if the landscape was flat because I felt the heat over my head. What affected me most was the toxic gas and the dust that it created after landing on the ground. I smelled blood as I was breathing and felt pain in my chest but I carried on until I found other people. Fortunately, there was an escape route that had been paved by those who normally went for food. This helped everyone to leave the danger zone without being injured despite the surprising nature of the attack and the numerous bullets and bombs shot. Carefully, we found our way out of the mountainous area and headed for the flat land where the LRA leader Joseph Kony was.

# 11

# Reunion with the Arabs

*"It was in this place that I realised I was expecting a second child."*

After that serious attack in Apwap, we followed Joseph Kony and his group to the low land where we had stayed before the Iron Fist operation. It took us one week to get there. We found that the relationship between the Arabs and the LRA had improved and so they began donating arms and food like sugar, wheat flour, grains, cooking oil and others, as they had been doing before. I appreciated this so much because it strengthened most of us who were starved for a long time while in the cold mountain ranges of Imatong. I was also happy that I was going to rest from the constant climbing of steep hills among hostile tribes. It was in this place that I realised I was expecting a second child. This was not easy for me, especially after reflecting on how those who had more than one child suffered during the 2002 Iron Fist operation, but I had no option other than to carry the child.

This new place came to be known as *Wat Odwogo*, (our relationship is restored) after the relation between the LRA and the Arabs was mended. This raised security hopes to the

LRA who even started building semi-permanent structures in which we were involved in the cutting of grass for roofing. We supplemented the food from the Arabs with the one from our gardens that we had planted before Operation Iron Fist. Crops like pigeon peas and sorghum had grown amidst weeds, and so we got enough to sustain us for a short period. Since we were located along the Kit River that was well known by the Ugandan soldiers as the only source of water that the LRA used domestically, we got scared that the UPDF would sneak back to Sudan to attack us again. Indeed, this was what happened.

One day some of the LRA soldiers who had gone for patrol brought back a report that the Ugandan soldiers were heading towards our camp. An order was given to burn all the huts as we evacuated at dawn to start living a mobile life making it difficult for the UPDF to find us. This was not an easy life to live as it involved moving from place to place, with heavy loads on heads and every time one had to be on guard for everyone's safety like keeping quiet, or reporting to the operation room anything that was a threat to the LRA.

We started living a life like that of wild animals in isolated plains in silence to avoid being noticed by the UPDF soldiers. When it was time for moving, the situation was even worse for me because of the load I was bearing. I had to carry my first born on my back and a load on my head. By the time we reached the next position, the piece of cloth that I used for tying the baby on my back had pressed hard on my belly and being pregnant I was very uncomfortable. This was coupled with the hot sun and the fatigue of moving for a long distance. It was a burden to me and even others who were lame. It was a dry season in March, characterised by strong sunshine with hot sunny days. Leaves had fallen off trees and most of the seasonal rivers were dry. Before camping, we first got a source of water that was adequate for the population of about five hundred people.

It was in March 2003 when a large number of LRA left Sudan for Uganda and only the disabled, the pregnant women and a few soldiers remained. I happened to be among those who remained in Sudan. I was left with two boys and girls as the rest of my bush family members left. These people helped me with carrying my baby and luggage, searching for food to eat and fetching water. But as the case was, to be on the safer side, we had to keep on moving from place to place in order to dodge the UPDF and the Arabs again.

One day we sneaked and crossed the main Juba Road to go and settle somewhere we could not be traced easily. By then, we had no food to eat and were feeding on wild plants growing by the river banks. From there, we got a safer position and stayed in one place for about three weeks. After that, we transferred to another place where we stayed for three days. The location seemed satisfactorily secure. It was located near a big water body and far away from the main road. Construction of semi-permanent buildings started again but food was scarce. My two 'girls' would wake up very early in the morning and go hunting for wild vegetables from the bush. They would come back at around 11am with whatever they had gathered. Among them was a very bitter plant that resembled a type of vegetable that from home was called *alaju* in Lango and *lalaa* in Acholi. Another was a plant that we discovered there called *oyoro*. This one cannot become tender no matter how long it is cooked. It was later ground with a grinding stone to make it softer. Another thing that they brought was raw pawpaw that we peeled and cooked for sauce. To make our lives better, we started digging in the month of May around our new homes and planted sim-sim, sorghum and vegetables. But this did not help us in time, except for the vegetables, because the rest of the crops took too long to mature.

On June 23rd 2003, I gave birth to a baby girl. From then on, everything that concerns her concerns me. What I realised is the father did not like her, but instead liked her brother. I will live to remember the way she cried. She started crying when she was less than a week old to an extent that I just looked on without any move to make her quiet as I had used all means to silence her. In the night she cried while I had sleepless nights. And instead of growing, she kept on reducing in size because of either starvation or a lot of crying. During the day, she slept and cried in the night until sweat covered her whole body. Even if I rocked her, she still cried. All this gave me a lot of stress that contributed to my weakness. At times I would let her cry as I did not have any other alternative. I did not know what was wrong with her. She would even cry for over thirty minutes non-stop.

Despite my condition, I did not give up. I kept on struggling here and there to see that I got a better means of surviving. Together with my two 'girls', we cut logs for burning charcoal. I was weak due to inadequate food since even the wild vegetables had become scarce due to the high demand. At times when there was nothing to eat, we made 'dry' tea and drank it without sugar. This in turn made us hungrier. But we struggled and cut logs that were enough to burn five bags of charcoal. We later carried these on our heads to sell to the Arabs in order to obtain some dura millet and salt. The transaction took place in Nicitu II near Juba highway, close to the barracks belonging to the Sudanese soldiers in Nicitu.

By this time, most people had grown thin and when you looked at a friend's face, the first thing you noticed were the cheekbones. Other people even died of starvation. One man who was commonly known as John perished. The one thing that kept us hopeful was the fact that we had planted some crops that would rescue us from hunger at some point. The only thing that we prayed for was security so that we could harvest what we had sown.

This situation made some of the LRA soldiers penetrate villages that were occupied by Sudanese, and they robbed them of their crops from the garden. This again spoilt the relationship between the Arabs and the LRA. It also made it easy for them to link with the UPDF who were searching for the LRA rebels. Later in July, a group from Uganda spearheaded by an LRA leader entered Sudan, and this gave us a lot of hope of surviving. With him were commanders like John and other brigade commanders. They came and saw our situation and organised to loot food from the Sudanese. That is how we were rescued from dying of hunger. This stand-by brought with them plenty of looted foodstuffs like sorghum, *sim-sim*, and goats that were slaughtered. This gave us the strength to move back to the Imatong ranges where we met Vincent Otti. That was when the idea of going back to Uganda came up.

I was weak and could not move on. The sorghum that had been brought helped me but I still felt weak though I had food for at least a week. We had started the journey when my baby was just one month old. She learnt to sit, crawl and finally walked at the age of ten months, and we were still on the move. When I moved, I would feel as if my hip bones were not in their right positions. No one had massaged me well when I gave birth. After giving birth, one was supposed to be massaged with hot water and oil for about one week to ensure that the hip bones that were dislocated during delivery go back to their normal state since there was no medication. I felt pain when I jumped over any pothole. When moving through thick grass, I found difficulty in overcoming its strength due to my body weakness. I also developed rashes because of the rough grass that brushed against my body.

We finally reached the Imatong ranges for the second time, but there was hardly any food in this place. Most civilians had fled their villages after their first experience with the conflict. We started surviving on sim-sim from the gardens of the few local inhabitants. We harvested, dried and made paste from it, and ate it with cassava leaves. We preserved the cassava root tubers for future use. The food was tasteless without salt, but we ate it in order to survive.

We stayed there for three months and then went down to where we had been before (near Juba) and another lot of stand-bys were sent to go and raid one of the pastoral tribes in Sudan to bring with them back herds of cattle. Before they went, they were assured by the LRA leader that all would be well with them. They brought three hundred herds of cattle with them. These were distributed to all households for slaughter. People cooked and ate all kinds of dishes that could be prepared from beef. After five days, another set of cows for slaughter was distributed. Beef became the only source of food that we survived on, but we kept on shifting positions for fear that these pastoralists would follow their cattle. Indeed, they came two times and the two parties engaged in a serious exchange of fire that involved loss of life on both sides. Commanders like Jimmy lost their lives. This act of raiding worsened the relationship between the LRA and the Arabs, so the best option was to make those who could move leave that area for the Imatong ranges again. We left with the remaining cattle, about one hundred of them, but things did not go well this time because the UPDF had occupied most areas in the ranges. That's where the idea of proceeding to Uganda came in. To me this was a surprise because since my arrival in Sudan on the 12th of December 1996, I had never been allowed to go back to Uganda. It was now April 2004.

# 12

## Back to Uganda

*"Please keep me alive so that I see my people if it is your wish."*

My journey back to Uganda began in April 2004. Our overall commander was Brigadier Vincent Otti. Then, the LRA could not stay in one place in Sudan like before because a large number of government troops were pursuing them. We were in the Imatong Mountains when Kony gave the order that everyone would return to Uganda. Immediately we headed for Atebi River, a very big river that separated Sudan from Uganda.

When we were told that we were coming back to Uganda, I had mixed feelings. First of all, I was scared of the situation in Uganda as narrated by those who had come before as awful. Those who had gone with Otti to Sudan said the situation was terrible, that many people had lost and were still losing their lives as a result of intensive military operation on the LRA by the Ugandan government. There was always constant fighting using helicopter gunships and infantry. Many people lost their lives because they could not hide well. These fighters could not differentiate the soldiers from the civilians. All those who stayed in the bush were killed as long as they were not able to hide well or run for their lives.

On the other hand, I was happy that it would be my chance to get my freedom from captivity and go to school again. I always dreamt of going back to school, but in my dreams, I was late for class or found the exams to be very difficult. With my mixed feelings, I gathered my few belongings and my two children and moved on. Those who were experienced kept on updating us on how to run and hide from helicopter gunships for safety. They told us that when a gunship comes, we should not try to hide under big trees because that's one of the areas they suspect rebels to be hiding. We were warned not to wear bright colored clothes but rather colors that resembled the environment. When the place was green, you had to have something green or black so the person in the plane would see you as a natural object and wouldn't aim there.

When hiding, one was supposed to hide his or her fingernails and forehead because they shine. They could be magnified from the aircraft and would show that there was a human being hiding within. You had to first hide your head. It was hard to hide the faces of the children even when you had hidden yours because the children didn't know why their mothers want them to do it. Possibly they may have thought the mother was playing a game, yet she was trying to save their lives. It was a risky game but I followed the procedure. I hid whenever I heard the sound of gunships or helicopters approaching from a distance. I learnt some of the tactics from Uganda in action and on my own. The journey to the Atebi

River was as long as I had thought it would be. Before we got there, some SPLA soldiers fought with the LRA at the riverside. They had gone fishing and at the same time spying. The LRA found them smoking fish and took all their fish after they had taken off. Unfortunately, they took information to the Ugandan government. The UPDF were always patrolling the area while monitoring where the LRA was heading to.

We moved for half a day at a terrible speed that I could not keep up with. At around 11 am the temperature had risen so high, and I was finding it difficult to move due to the heat. I learnt that topographically Sudan is situated at a higher altitude than Uganda because we kept going downhill as we were heading to Uganda. We kept on moving, crossing rivers, hills and valleys. When I looked ahead, I saw valleys and hoped there was water but there was nothing except empty river beds. I had to cross and move ahead in the hope of getting another water source, yet I badly needed it. It was tiresome to move on a hot day. Whoever got tired rested, but those who were fit and had nothing to carry moved non-stop and were the first to reach the position.

There were very many of us, about five hundred or more. These included a few people with babies and ladies without guns, but the majority were well armed men. The mothers only carried something small as luggage and their babies, and they were to stay in Uganda for safety as Sudan could not be lived in anymore. I followed them in humility, as I saw that they were much stronger, well armed and experienced in the field of hiding from the gunships and in the military. I humbled myself and moved with the group led by Vincent

Otti and other prominent commanders like Brigadier Kenneth Banya, Major Kwoyelo Latoni, Buk Budema and many other young officers of lower ranks.

This was a very large group but was split up for easy movement and safety on reaching Uganda. My group was led by Vincent Otti as the overall commander, alongside Kenneth Banya and Kwoyelo, and was positioned in Gulu. All these commanders had their bodyguards and their women, and in all we were about fifty in number. Most were armed male soldiers consisting of mature men and some young boys between the ages of twelve and fifteen. There were a few ladies like me with babies.

I remember how frightened I was during the five months in Uganda. We stayed in a place called Olamnyur, Zoka forest, along the river Wiceri and around Kilak hill. These were then deadly places to survive in. They were always occupied by government soldiers who were always on the hunt for the LRA. Our party thus was always tense most of the time and on a look out for the UPDF at all time. Moreover, this was forested area. Keeping alert was of essence.

On arrival at River Atebi, the first thing we did was prepare lunch. Again, we had no flour, so we had to grind the sorghum that we were carrying to make flour for making bread. I began to look for appropriate stones (*nyakidi*) for grinding, but I searched in vain. That was what we used to do whenever we reached any position. In order to have a meal, each one had to participate in its preparation in one way or the other in order to save time, since we were always given limited time to prepare food.

In my position, there were about ten ladies, six of whom had children. My daughter was the noisiest. She used to cry a lot, and this was a threat to our security when we started the journey to Uganda. I was not allowed to participate in domestic activities except when she was asleep or quiet. I then had to light the fire to begin cooking some pieces of smoked meat that we carried from Sudan. Suddenly, I heard the sound of a helicopter gunship at around 1 pm and sensed danger just as we had been forewarned. I got up at once and started collecting and putting together some of the cooking utensils that were scattered. This was the most important item to any LRA member. Whoever left her saucepans risked severe punishment or even loss of life.

In about fifteen minutes, the whole position was in total confusion. Somebody was either taking cover, or fleeing from from the position for their dear lives as the sound of helicopter gunships drew nearer. I called for Irene, the girl who was carrying my older child, and we moved away quickly as two helicopter gunships were approaching. No sooner had we found our way to an empty river bed than the gunship began bombing. We hid holding our chests in prayer for two things: that no infantry should find us and that the gunship should not begin shooting our area.

After two to three good hours of bombardment, the gunships left, but only after causing serious destruction. One woman, Aluku, a wife to one of Joseph Kony's bodyguards called Ocan, lost her child who was shot from behind as she was hiding. It happened in our first position along the shore of the Atebi River. This was so painful to watch, as I witnessed and felt the pain of losing a child. From then on, I realised that even the lives of my own children were uncertain. She hid but did not hide her baby well enough. The baby had been right on her back and died. All the fifty cows were bombarded.

Many people were injured and others went their own way to join other groups that belonged to the LRA. When the bombardment was over, we moved to another position. My bush family now included the boys we were taking care of (fellow abductees), the ladies (three were my co-wives) and the others who were temporarily staying with us. These were the only people that were close to me, and we stayed as a family for we shared all our good and bad moments together. We kept on moving along the river Atebi for three days in order to dodge the Ugandan forces, but no day went by without us being bombarded. That alone made me predict how dangerous and risky life was going to be in Uganda. This was because the Ugandan soldiers were already aware of the direction the LRA was heading and this was an attempt to block the border.

We crossed the junction where River Aswa joins a certain river late in the evening at around 6 pm on the third day of heavy bombardment. The water was below the knees, fresh and flowing slowly as I drew some in my five litre jerry can for future use. At this time, I was already tired and stressed, out yet we had been briefed by Vincent Otti that we should forget about resting that night since we had to cross the risky Sudan-Uganda border. In my mind, I imagined a deadly situation of entering an ambush at night when everyone was tired, with little knowledge of which direction to take. I wondered whether anybody would survive bullets or death. I moved but was lifeless, as I remembered an attack seven years ago in a 1996 night in an area called *Tee Got Atoo*. A bullet had passed over my head and I had felt the heat burn my head and saw the light from the bullet as it was passing. I felt and saw how painful an attack was at night since survival was narrow.

When that day's struggle of hiding and dodging gunships ended, I moved together with my bush family members and sat somewhere under tall, thorny trees after crossing the Atebi River. We spent a night by the cold but failed to get a good position to rest for the night because of the scanty vegetation that could not hide the large number of LRA from the UPDF air force. We were many and everyone struggled to get the thickiest vegetation that would cover us from aircrafts. I cannot forget that day's bombardment. I believe I survived by God's mercy by hiding in a valley by the riverside together with some other LRA members. From the valley, the gunship would pass over us as it prepared to drop bombs, I watched from a distance the damage being caused by the gunship. What almost took away my breath was the terrible sound of a bombarding aircraft and the fact that it was turning from a point that was just above my hiding place. After that, I moved along the river with very little hope for life because I was afraid that it would come back again.

On the second day, we moved in the wilderness without coming across many obstacles like rivers or hills. This was flat land with short vegetation. All the LRA members under the command of Brigadier Vincent Otti were on the move in the same direction heading southeast from where we had crossed the Atebi River. We walked in an extended manner to ease movement and taking cover in case of the arrival of the UPDF aircraft. I followed them because they knew the direction to Uganda. We found a python and fortunately it was dead. Vincent Otti said it was a bad sign. Others said something bad was going to happen. This discouraged me the more.

We kept on moving because we could not go back to Sudan, even though we were aware that danger lay ahead. At midday, another helicopter gunship came. Since very many LRA soldiers were scattered in an open area, they were noticed. We made an attempt to hide but the two helicopter gunships still bombarded us. The LRA began to shoot at it with an anti-aircraft gun but it retaliated and cannonaded those with the anti-aircraft guns. The operators were wounded and even those standing close to them lost their lives. Many people were wounded and others separated from the group as it seemed risky to move in a large group. After the gunship had finished bombarding, the operation room gave positions near Atebi River. I boiled *nyoi* for the next day.

After the second attack on the same day, a ritual was performed. Joseph Kony sent a message that everyone in the group was cursed and so a cleansing ritual would be performed. Leaves were spread across the path and everyone was to step on them while pleading to God in any way for protection. I also stepped on the leaves and passed to purify myself. After that, we went to rest in our positions earlier than usual. We ate our packed food while John our bush husband briefed us on our journey. We were going to move that whole night and the following morning in order to cross the border where no one was expected to stop or knock anything. Even those with babies were told to make sure they were quiet.

I knew instantly that there was danger. I made sure my noisy baby was quiet by doing whatever she wanted. Since she was on my back, when she woke up, I would quickly remove her and breastfeed then put her on my back again as soon as she fell asleep. My luggage remained on my head. This burden sat on my head for nearly two days. This caused a burning pain on my head and on my neck. This was even worsened by the long period we spent standing on the line as we waited for the stand-bys who had gone ahead to check out the safety of the border to come back to. In a single line, we would make about two to three steps and then stop for a while until we crossed the border in dead silence in the middle of the night.

This slow movement made me more tired and I kept on dozing while standing in the line. From then, I realised how important a night's rest is in everyone's life. I yearned to sleep but had to keep awake for the sake of my life. That was the second straight day we passed on empty stomachs. We continued moving in one line in stony, irregular landscape on a dark night. We were told to move together with our family members to avoid getting lost at night. From this painful experience, I realised that for the sake of life anybody can do anything to keep alive.

That evening before we crossed the border, Brigadier Vincent Otti gave this order: "There is no turning back even if we get soldiers. Nobody should run away but fight until we cross by hook or crook." We had to move carefully but fast to avoid being noticed by the UPDF in the process of sneaking across the border. There was only a very small gap that was safe. We were told not to turn back even when there was fire exchange, so we carried our almost lifeless bodies in a single line.

Then, we were still a group of about five hundred fighters as we had come from Sudan. When we were lining up to cross the border, I was with my co-wives, and all the fifteen boys that we were keeping, and John as well. In my heart, I was pleading with God to let me cross the border when my children and I are alive, even if I am a sinner. I was like, "God, the way I came to exist in this dangerous place was out of my control. Please keep me alive so that I see my people if it is your wish."

We went to a place and found dry leaves that had been spread on the ground for sleeping by soldiers who were waiting to ambush the LRA. I saw fire in the distance ahead of us. I heard male voices just a few metres away from us, but we passed them quietly amidst cut barbed wire and dry leaves. I was lost in fear and my hands were cold and sweaty because at any moment in this strange land that I had little knowledge of, my life could end. This made me feel feverish and all my joints ached. But on the other hand, I was pleased that we managed to cross the border peacefully into my homeland, the one that I hadn't seen since 1996, without finding the UPDF who were commonly known as *Olalu*.

We moved and reached a village in West Nile (Madi) very late in the night. The hungry LRA fighters stormed the village and started looting items like chicken, groundnuts and turkeys. The villagers easily noticed our presence because the rebels had scattered all over the village, which of course was strange to them. Such people made us lose the track in the night and we stood waiting for those who could take us to the direction where the main leading team of operation room was heading to.

We moved the whole night and reached an area where people had planted crops, but most of them had fled their homes after realising that the LRA was approaching their village. Some Madi were abducted, while others ran away even after being captured without fearing that they could easily be shot in the process of running.

## Hiding from the UPDF in Uganda

I was extremely tired and hungry when we reached Bibia trading centre and crossed a tarmac road at around 7.30am I saw helicopters flying from a distance ahead of us, high in the sky on a cloudy morning. It was monitoring every movement of the LRA from above. At Bibia, the LRA looted very many things from the shops. I managed to pick a green basin for bathing my babies in, put my bag in it, and carried it on my head. The never-ending journey continued.

For safety in case the gunships attacked, we were then divided into groups of four brigades and I was in Otti's group. There was one thing that was always kept secret, the direction of movement or where the RV (secret meeting place of LRA groups) was going to take place. The vegetation was scanty with short trees and grass, as it had just started to grow after being burnt in the dry season. I was bored never ending journey. But we kept on moving amidst the short trees on a very hot, sunny day to the rendezvous point known to only the top commanders. I rested whenever I got tired just like others were doing, but I made sure that I caught up with the rest in my group to avoid getting lost in a place that I was not familiar with. People were scattered all over the bush but moving in the same direction to the secret meeting place.

This village we were moving in had scattered settlements of grass-thatched huts and a vast grazing pasture land with many herds of cattle grazing freely without anyone attending to them. Grazing land separated the homesteads. We moved towards a certain hill. At around midday, we heard helicopters bombarding from a distance. Some gunmen also shot at us and we changed the direction of our movement from the north to the west. From there, we realised that the government troops were following the other LRA groups that had split from us.

They followed us up to Aringapii in Madi where the LRA groups were to meet. They were either always informed or traced the trails of LRA. At around 1pm, we continued moving, towards the Ayugi River for water. We had been looking for water for two days. People picked cassava and other items on the way but we could not sit down and cook them to eat because there was no water. Fortunately we reached the Ayugi River at around 2 pm. Extremely excited to see water, I hurriedly dipped myself into the mass of cold water in the river and drew some in a five-litre jerrycan. On hearing a helicopter gunship approaching, I quickly crossed the river, targeting a banana plantation for a hiding place. I looked back across the river, and saw a majority of people still left behind also taking cover as fast as they could under the few shrubs that were there.

Watching and hearing from the banana plantation, I was lost in the world of fear as I monitored the movement of the dangerous helicopter. I saw the gunship over my head as it was turning to go and cannonade those on the other side of the river. The sound of the bombarding gunships made me quake in my hiding place, and my nine-month-old daughter kept on looking into my face wondering at my weird actions. As the gunship was busy bombarding, the infantry was approaching because I could hear gunshots nearing from all directions behind me. I knew for sure that this was dangerous, because the UPDF soldiers had a habit of moving nearer and waiting until the helicopter had completed its mission before advancing towards LRA soldiers when they were not aware and seriously firing at them. The end result was massive loss of lives or injury on the side of the rebels. After analysing all this and the fact that I was too weak to carry the luggage that I had anymore, I removed everything from the bag that was heavy, remained with what I could carry, and joined the rest like Captain Kwoyelo who were familiar with the area. At an unbelievable speed, we made our way among the short trees and grass along the Ayugi River. I think the UPDF soldiers had laid an ambush along the river because as I was moving towards the river a bullet passed over my head. It did not touch me, and I immediately changed my direction of movement because I realised danger was ahead. This really scared me as I hurriedly turned away from the direction of the river and disappeared in the bushes.

Most of the people who were behind me were injured. I also lost a schoolmate called Louisa who died at the spot. She climbed a tree to hide from gunships, not knowing she was getting nearer to the plane. She was focused on and shot. Earlier on in the morning, she had told me, "These girls in Otti's home look down on us because we have no gumboots, as if they bought them with their own money. If any of them confronts me on that issue, I will abuse them." I had advised her to ignore them.

At that point, each person minded only about his or her own safety and life. My son and his babysitter also took a different route that I didn't know and survived narrowly, from what the babysitter narrated to me later after we met in the evening. She was far away from where I was hiding. Whenever exchange of fire took place or there was cannonading by war planes, each person in the LRA ran his or her own way in order to survive. Otherwise, there was a high risk of losing one's life in the process of trying to save it if very many people were to be in one place.

We moved as if we were going to the north but then came back in order to dodge the plane. Unfortunately, that area had little vegetation that could hide us from the gunmen in the plane, and the deadly gunships were approaching again. They were guided by a white aircraft that did not drop bombs. We called it *Awany*, the commander that was then in charge of air operations. At a certain point we stopped moving all together because this plane was monitoring all our movements. We were followed in every corner until we hid ourselves in the short, leafless, thorny shrubs that were there.

Ground soldiers were also advancing towards us. I could hear their gunshots from a distance. This was the second time on the same day that both the soldiers and gunships were closing in on us. I hid and covered myself and the baby with my baby's shawl to avoid being noticed from the aircraft, the shawl was greenish in color. The baby cried because it did not want to be covered on a hot day but I held her tight to prevent her from making any shaking movement in the shrubs we were hiding in because that would have been the end of us. I held her tightly on my chest, but I could hear gunshots coming closer and again from our side, planes were also bombing. I looked to see whether they were coming closer to us, when the gunship had moved away for a while. The gunship dropped a bomb between me and my co-wife who was hiding a few metres from me. I was afraid that my co-wife and her daughter had died as that area was dusty and with poor visibility.

While all this was happening, violent black ants (*kalang*) gathered around my feet, but I dared not to move in order to save our lives. I had to let them bite me to avoid being hit by a bomb. A boy who stayed at our home escaped being hurt by a grenade that was dropped from the plane near his hiding place. The pin that must be removed first before it explodes had not been removed, so it failed to explode and so that was his luck.

We crossed Ayugi River from a different point. However I was low in spirit fearful of another ambush. I could neither see my son and the baby sitter nor any member of my family. The immediate thought that came into my mind was that they were all dead as a result of that day's heavy bombardment. I kept on asking other LRA members who were arriving one by one, who told me they were alive. They had run away in a different direction after crossing the border. With the fatigue of constant movement for three consecutive days, the weak ones like me were moving at a slower pace while the strong ones moved faster. This is what brought about the splitting in the group. Many people were wounded and others died on the spot and I thought my bush family members were all affected. Later on when they came back from different directions they had taken for safety, I was delighted to see them.

In the LRA family was so important in one's life because these were the people who would stand by you in case of problems, like nursing you if you were wounded. The boys would be the ones to bring food that we survived on and so their absence was costly in terms of hunger and lack of someone to send in case you were in need. But this depended on how the ladies treated the boys. Mistreatment meant a bad relationship and suffering from hunger.

After being given the positions for resting, we were to leave at around 1 am in order to cross the risky Atiak-Bibia main road. Luckily, night clashes between the LRA and the UPDF were not common. This was the best time to cross that road. All my family members managed to be around and survived injury from bullets. That night I was so tired but almost failed to fall asleep because of fear of what the next day would be like. At around midnight Buk Budema, who was to spearhead the stand-bys in crossing the Atiak-Bibia Road, woke us up.

On a cold dark night of April 2004, we set off through steep, stony and irregular landscape and were cautioned not to make any noise. The person who was leading us told us to go to the west but John insisted that we go to the south. This was not an argument because it's a culture in the LRA that a commander's words be obeyed as it was believed that God speaks through elders and leaders. And that was how we survived entering an ambush that night.

We were coming from the south. The one taking the lead kept on insisting we go westwards. We then went back and followed John's suggestion. Just after we had diverted, UPDF soldiers heard our footsteps, and according to where the gunshots were coming from, we were heading towards them. Everyone was afraid and ran to a safer direction without firing back a single bullet. They began to shoot at us but did not know which direction we were taking because it was dark. We were near them and the bullets flew above us. We dodged them and did not follow the direction where the gunshots were heading. I was very frightened because it reminded me of the previous day's bombardment that I had survived narrowly. I knew that to live in Uganda was not easy. That was the night that the big group that was led by Brigadier Vincent Otti split up under various commands to operate in the different areas allocated to them in Uganda.

We moved until dawn but finally we we reached the main road that was in a valley and both sides were steep, so it was difficult to climb up to the other side. My only prayer was that we don't find soldiers or get involved in an exchange of fire. We crossed very fast and climbed over to the other side of the road. We moved through forests and thick bushes, finally we ended in Olamnyu with Kwoyelo as our guide. He showed us where to get cassava and how to survive there. My group consisted of Otti's, Kwoyelo's and John's families.

We had to be on guard in case the planes came. The cassava that was brought was watery and others were spongy. It had stayed so long in the soil after it was planted. Those who had planted it had fled to the camps. We ate it raw rather than lighting a fire during the daytime, and informed the war crafts that were ever in the air of our presence by the smoke from our fire. By this time most of the civilians in Northern Uganda were in Internally Displaced Person's (IDP) camps. Any strange thing that showed the presence of people in places like forests or in the wilderness made the Ugandan soldiers eager to know which people were there. I was always thinking about how I was going to survive. I had to be alert all the time and always found a way of making the babies quiet. When people were sent to get cassava, they would find that soldiers had just passed looking for where the LRA was. Life was risky and it was hard to believe that one was going to survive. This is sometime between April and May 2004.

The next place we went to was the Kilak hills (*Te Kilak.*) This place had rocks and were thick forests. It was not far from the Madi, a neighbouring tribe to the Acholi. The vegetation was thick and one could not be seen by those in the army aircrafts that were ever in the air searching for the LRA. It was isolated in the jungle far away from settlements. When we were going, we found so many trails of soldiers hunting for the LRA rebels. They believed *Te Kilak* was a suitable hiding place for the LRA because of its vegetation.

We stayed here for a month under difficult conditions. There was no food and we survived on palm nuts (*tugu*). We were not allowed to hit them hard in preparation for eating for fear of being noticed by the UPDF in case they were passing nearby. We were to hit them stealthily. To make matters worse, the boys hid some of the foodstuffs they brought and so we always ran out off supplies. We were given food that lasted only for two days. They also always took long to return from where they went to gather food. This meant that by the time food was brought, we would have starved a lot. We hid every morning whenever we heard the sound of any war craft in the air. This created tension and fear all the time as we could not live freely. One day my son told me, "mum, I have red shoes and if the plane sees them on my legs, won't I be hit by the bomb from the plane?" I assured him that that wouldn't happen. He was four years old then and spoke as though he was predicting how he would be killed.

There was only one meal a day for everyone, including the children. The little food that was cooked had to be taken to the leaders and also given to the children. I would eat very little and survive on the *tugu*.

# 13

## The day I will never forget

*"I lost my son and co-wife and I almost lost my life."*

One of my worst days was the 17th of July 2004 when I lost my son and my co-wife, and I almost lost my life too. Such a tragedy had never occurred to me. On this day, some stand-bys had gone to loot food from Pabbo, a village in Gulu. It was a fine morning with the bright sun in the cloudless sky. At around 8 am, a boy who was set aside to see if soldiers were coming came running to inform the rest of us who were in the defense that some soldiers were advancing towards us. That information sent the whole defense into quick reflex motion. All of a sudden, people started grabbing what they could very fast from all directions and started running to the west since the UPDF were coming from the east.

I quickly put my baby on my back. My baby sitter Irene did the same with my first born who was then almost five years old, and we rushed to where we thought was safe using a foot path. We reached Unyama River around 11.00 am and started crossing the slow flowing river while stepping on stones that were on the river bed. As soon as I had crossed I heard the sound of a helicopter gunship, and I knew this was danger. Then, while either the gunship was cannonading or the exchange of fire was taking place, it was very hard to trace and protect another person. Each of us knew where and how to flee from such incidents and we would meet ahead if it was at all possible.

On realising that the rebels were there, the aircraft started instantly bombarding the people who were ahead. Unfortunately, a man called Ojara Pope, one of my bush husband's bodyguards would later to tell me one of these bombs happened to land on my son, his baby sitter and my co-wife. According to him, the aircraft found these people in an open place with less vegetation, my co-wife went to hide under the only bushy shrub that was nearby, she sent my babysitter away. In the process of running to find a new hiding place, the babysitter was seen from the aircraft and a bomb was dropped directly on them, splitting them into pieces and injuring my co-wife. My son's head was blown up on a tree and his body disappeared in the dark smoke.

After the gunship had left, some commanders in the LRA told everyone to move ahead faster as the infantry was in pursuit. So we rushed in the direction we were shown to cross the Atiak road before an ambush was set though our calculation went wrong.

We then reached a place that was not so far from the main road, the helicopter gunships started moving in the air and we started hiding again. But as we were doing so, I saw a wild animal that looked like an antelope coming from the direction we had come from. It went ahead of us, came back and encircled us then went back to where it came from. This was the same route that the UPDF used to reach us.

When we were being pursued, we were advised to keep moving ahead whenever the gunship was turning to begin cannonading to avoid being caught by the advancing soldiers. We kept moving ahead, and at one point I started hearing deep, unusual male voices from behind. I knew these were the government soldiers, or *Olalu* as commonly known by the LRA. Without wasting time, I hurried ahead, and left some of my friends behind because of fear that if I was caught my chances of surviving would be narrow. In less than five minutes, two helicopter gunships were in the air just over my head. I got confused when the gunship was so close to me. I could clearly see the gunmen, very ready to shoot. This scared the life out of me because soldiers were even shooting at us from behind so I could not retreat. I had to force my way ahead where the war crafts had started dropping bombs. What came to my mind was to leave behind my belongings that I was carrying on my head. And as soon as the aircrafts started dropping bombs after locating where I was, I threw my luggage away and ran to take cover under a tree with my baby on my back. I realised this area was dangerous and started crawling away. I had just moved when a bomb landed. All I felt were soil particles pouring on us as I continued to crawl away. A second bomb fell close to me and I knew I was being monitored from the plane. I kept moving forward.

Unfortunately, I reached a point that had less vegetation cover which could no longer hide me. I got up, shook away the soil particles, and started running openly from soldiers who were seriously shooting and from the two gunships that were alternately bombing where I was. I got tired after covering only a short distance as my chest heated up, and I started smelling blood. I looked back after I heard bullets being fired at me, but I did not give up on moving. I kept on moving towards a valley. I did not care about being wounded. All I wanted was to get as far away as possible from the pursuing soldiers.

As I was running down into the valley, I saw a girl who had survived running after me and I stopped, waited for her and we went down together. She told me that her friend had been shot, and in the process of dying, she had jumped on her and held her tightly. She kept on pleading with the dead one to stop holding on to her tight not knowing that she was dead. So she forcefully moved away from her and ran after me, and those who were behind her were captured by the UPDF.

As we were moving, she kept on insisting that we go south where the Atiak main road was, but I refused because I was hearing soldiers shouting from there. We crossed another river and went west where the soldiers had started shooting from. I thought it would be safe there. After ten minutes, we reached a point where we could hear soldiers shouting, others cutting trees, and others shooting bullets at some people who were running away. We were stranded and confused and so did not know which direction to follow. Then I told my colleague, "I cannot surrender to the UPDF because they have that anger in them, and most of them have this idea of raping women. Moreover, nobody knows their HIV status. I don't want to be a victim of gang rape. I will rather hide under that big tree and let them find because of my baby's noise or any such coincidence." I removed my baby from my back and checked if she was injured. I found my blouse covered with red dust that had gotten soaked in my sweat as I was crawling, but neither of us was wounded.

At around 5 pm on the 17th of July 2004, we were hiding under a tall, huge tree that was surrounded by dry, grey grass in great fear. It seemed like the soldiers had surrounded us because from the south, men were talking, shouting, raising an alarm, and yelling at the top of their voices. To the east, some soldiers were firing bullets at people who seemed to be on the run. Someone was also cutting a tree nearby, while a short distance from us I could hear someone who seemed to be wounded groaning in pain somewhere in the bush. To the north, I could hear footsteps of soldiers moving on dry grass and from my hiding place, I was extremely afraid.

Meanwhile, my hungry daughter was crying at the top of her voice for breast milk, which was not adequate for her. In my heart I asked, "God, are you going to make these lusty soldiers discover where I am because of my own child's noise? If not then let this child eat these particles of soil and keep quiet." So I picked some soil from the ground and gave it to her, and she ate them and fell asleep. We remained still until 8pm when it was dark for we believed that both advancing armed forces would be resting. We would then be safe to cross the empty river and find a place to rest for the night. I plucked some leaves from a tree and laid them down for a bed. I reflected on how that day was for me before I slept. I had lost my son and his baby sitter, my co-wife, and had almost lost my life. At that moment, I did not know what to do.

The following morning, a cock's crow from a nearby camp that I was later told was Atiak - Pawel woke me up. I got up very fast on hearing this and woke up my colleague as well so that we could leave before my baby began crying again. It was still dark when we set off following the direction of the moon as our guide in the hope of reaching the position that we had left the previous morning. As I was the one taking the lead, I moved cautiously and took one step at a time for the sake of our security while taking note of any slight sound from all directions.

I had moved less than 100 metres when I heard the strange sound of an object ahead of me getting up from my left side. I stopped for a moment to listen. I took another step ahead and heard the murmurs of male voices, and instantly realised that those were the UPDF soldiers in an ambush. I signaled to my friend and as fast as we could, we hurried back and away from them in another direction. We were able to recover our previous days trail as day light broke. This was a relief to us since we were gambling with directions. I was surprised by the foot marks of the very many soldiers who had followed only the two of us when we ran away from the war crafts. They had failed to trace our whereabouts. We followed one of the three pronounced trails and went down to cross a river and found a man lowering his hook in the water to catch fish. When he saw us, all of us, including him, got scared. He dropped his hook in the water and ran for his dear life, as we also found our way as fast as we could in a different direction.

Heading for the previous day's scene, we passed through thick grass cover that was wet from the morning dew. This made us so wet that by the time we reached where I had thrown my luggage, we were all shivering from the cold. In my attempt to look for my belongings, we came across a lit fire, a sign that somebody was there. We heard a sound nearby made by someone who was running away from us after sensing us approaching. On realising that someone was there, I told my colleague that we should leave that place immediately for our safety for none of us knew the intentions of that person who had run away, leaving his cassava roasting by the lit fire.

We tried to figure out which way could lead us to the position that we had left before the attack in order to find some of the LRA soldiers who had gone for stand-by. We started off following the eastern direction where the sun had risen from. This led to some minor trail that we recognised as that of the LRA from the marks on the soles of their gumboots that appeared old in comparison to those of the UPDF that appeared new. Indeed this was true because we found particles of preserved cassava that had poured on the way, and we picked some and helped ourselves to them as we headed for Unyama River. This was where the first bombardment had taken place the day before. I wanted to reach the very spot where my son died but I failed to locate it, so I gave up and went to cross the river. We moved quietly and frightfully because we knew that government agents were always on these big rivers pretending to be fishermen. They later informed the UPDF immediately, and we were right. As I was entering the river, I saw two men seated in the water with their backs turned on the bank where we were approaching. When I saw them talking to each other, I turned back quietly and signaled my colleague who was behind to remain quiet. We then paved a way from another point to cross the river without being noticed by these men. This was at around midday, and it was successful.

We came to the main trail that we had followed the day before, and we found very many condoms thrown on the way by the UPDF soldiers as they were running after us. We got very scared but confirmed that indeed these soldiers raped the women they came across as they were conducting their operation. We branched off to rest in a valley afraid of bumping into them. Thereafter, we proceeded to where we hoped to meet those who had gone for stand-by. Fortunately, we found them also arriving one-by-one from where they were assigned to go. Their mission was not accomplished because of the tight security by the government soldiers. We set off together with these boys to meet another group of LRA from the Gilva Brigade. It was amongst this group where I found one of my co-wives. We stayed with them until we were handed over to Vincent Otti's group.

I stayed in Vincent Otti's group for about two months. On meeting him, he called me and my co-wife and said,

"John your husband, who has been captured by the UPDF is pleading that we should release you. Moreover, he is talking against the LRA. But you should put in mind that I don't have the power to set you free unless Joseph Kony gives me the order then I can do that. For now, do whatever we are doing."

This was the period when news reached home that I was dead. One commander called Okot Tingting who witnessed my son's death and other girls who saw me crawling to escape the cannonading of the helicopter gunship were captured together with John. They told my parents that I had died in that attack. My mum had already sent my death announcement over the radio, and this attracted relatives and friends for mourning at our place as I later learnt. However, one woman who had seen me a week before she escaped informed my parents, who were already organising to collect my corpse, that I was alive. You can imagine how people who had already given up and lost hope about my return abandoned mourning and continued asking God for my return alive and this led them into serious prayer for my safety and return, which came to pass.

# 14

# How I escaped from captivity

*"...Whenever the sun rose, all I was thinking of was whether it would set when I was still alive..."*

This was not an easy thing to do as it involved the risk of losing one's life. Many who tried escaping without a proper plan lost either their own lives or that of their families from home because those LRA soldiers who knew them traced them, burnt down their homes and killed their family members. More so, LRA commanders had brainwashed the abductees in a way that made it hard for them to abandon the rebel movement. A case in point is ours, where Joseph Kony himself assured the schoolgirls that were abducted from my school that we were already being taken as rebels so whoever escaped among us wouldn't be excused but killed. He said that since many UPDF soldiers had lost their lives in an attempt to rescue us from the rebels, they would not have any mercy on us.

In addition to that, eye witnesses told me about one of my schoolmates who was shot in the leg by the UPDF, but when she called for help and mentioned the name of our former school, she was ignored and later raped by all the UPDF soldiers in that battalion until she died. This was horrible to hear and it made me rethink. Much as I was suffering, I vowed not to pass through UPDF if I got the chance of escaping. My escape was not easy because I passed through stages that were both miraculous and risky, but with God's guidance and prayers from all those who were concerned, I made it through.

The first step was being allowed to come back to Uganda after seven years and the difficult conditions like the intensive operation that the Ugandan government launched against the LRA rebels made life in the bush much harder. For example, I was in Vicent Otti's group that was most wanted. So during our short stay in the Kilak Hills, we were tracked down and found. Consequently, we had to be on our toes in order to survive while being pursued by the UPDF. All these confirmed that our ways of thinking and plans are not the same as God's.

The only time we rested was at night when the other party was also doing so. You can imagine running from energetic, well-trained and well-fed soldiers on our empty stomachs, with regular, simultaneous attacks by both infantry and the air force. This became so constant I felt my life was uncertain. Whenever the sun rose, all I was thinking of was whether it would set when I was still alive. It reached an extent where we had to survive on wild plants called *adyebo* without salt or anything to accompany it. They were tasteless, light and could not generate the energy that we needed to keep running from the UPDF.

This was the kind of life I lived from my arrival in Uganda in April to late June 2004. As a result, I had grown thin and weak but what kept me moving was the fact that I was still alive, despite my horrible appearance. A lot of hair had fallen off from my head because of the luggage that I was ever carrying. My daughter was breastfeeding, nevertheless she grew thin and cried out due to inadequate breast milk. To the rebels, her noise, together with the ones of other babies, was a threat to their security. That's why I was always warned whenever she was cried. As a result, Vincent Otti gave an order that we be separated from his group so he could sneak unnoticed from the Kilak region.

It was in late August 2004 at midday when fifteen of us left after splitting from Vincent Otti's group, in the hope of meeting in another place. We were seven females (five having children), and the rest were men.

After separating, we crossed two rivers and rested on some rocks where we had the packed *nyoi* that we had prepared the previous day. After finishing, we carried on with the journey, but little did we know that an ambush was laid somewhere along our way. We continued through thick, tall, hairy grass. The weather was so hot that my baby started crying because of the heat. I removed her from my back, then started breastfeeding her while moving. We were moving in a single line, and I was the third. As we were approaching an empty river bed, I suddenly heard gunshots being fired at us. By then, the two people in front of me had already crossed the river.

On seeing the hands that were firing at us, I threw away the luggage I was carrying on my head and made my way through the empty river bed. Shaking in fear from the sound of the numerous bullets being fired at my colleagues who were still behind me, I found my way to the other side of another river that was safer. This time I had nothing apart from my baby on my back. At the scene of ambush, I heard voices of two babies that I recognised, the one of my co-wife who was immediately behind me when we were still moving in the line and the voice of one child that belonged to one of Kony's bodyguards called Quinto. All were crying at the same spot and I realised that either their mothers or they themselves had been wounded. I wanted to help them but fear couldn't let me so, I decided to run for my dear life.

Back to where I was, there was a boy called Kipindi who was leading us initially and was wounded on the leg after the ambush. When he saw me, he chased me away saying that my baby was ever noisy and if she started crying, soldiers would find us so fast. I pleaded with him to let me follow him since I did not know which direction to follow but he kept quiet. I followed him stealthily until I reached a river and stood on one side of the bank. He hid himself and I got scared and stood still thinking he was going to shoot me. Instead, he later called me and told me to cross the river carefully to avoid being seen by the UPDF soldiers. I joined him together with three other girls, and we became five in number.

We moved to the riverside upland where each one contributed whatever they had for the preparation of that evening's meal. Kipindi had a lighter. One girl from my position had a saucepan that had a hole drilled in it by a bullet while she was running away from UPDF. The other girl had some maize grains, and another had beans. Those are the things we survived on for three days. These girls prepared the meal, while I was set a distance from them because of my noisy baby who was a threat to their security. This was done so I could face the consequence of my baby's character as I would be the first to be attacked, giving them the opportunity to flee from danger.

For this same reason, these people kept trying to persuade me to accept to be hidden in the forest alone for the sake of their safety, and they would bring me food at my hiding place. I realised that it was a trick to get rid of me which would have been a risk on my side since I would not know which way to go in case they failed to check up on me and bring me food.

At around 6 pm, we came across very many farms where crops like beans, green peas, and some vegetables were being grown, and this was evidence that people were living close by. This was an Internally Displaced Persons (IDP) camp, where a group of LRA fighters had attacked a month earlier and done a lot of nasty things like killing and looting. Kipindi told me and one other girl to stay back in the forest while the three of them checked on the security of the area before we could join them. What instantly clicked in my mind was that this was another trick to get rid of me, so we moved closer to them and hid ourselves in a nearby bush where we were able to see whoever was moving without them noticing us. My thought became a reality when Stella, the girl I was with, confirmed to me that all along my colleagues had been planning to desert me, but she had been in my support. That's why they had decided to leave her with me.

After waiting for over two hours, we saw them coming but they were dodging us, thinking we were not seeing them. After they had vanished in a different direction, we secretly followed them by their footsteps up to their hiding place where they were removing beans from their pods. This was a big surprise to them since they thought they had gotten rid of us. We joined them in what they were doing while waiting for nightfall so we could sneak through the cultivated land to a safe zone.

We started the risky journey by crossing a swamp at around 8 pm in the evening and moved through a forest with thick, tall grass. We were under the leadership of Kipindi, who was the only one who knew the direction. In order to avoid being traced the following morning, we removed our gumboots when crossing any *shamba*. From our movement and judging from the noise made by those in the IDP camp and the lights from their fires, I sensed that we were moving around the camp. This was one of the IDP camps that Vincent Otti had attacked, so getting captured by any member of that community would have cost us our lives.

In the cold night we moved barefoot on rough objects. Thorns pricked the soles of my feet painfully, but I continued limping after my colleagues. It so happened that one girl hit herself and fell down, thereby making a loud sound that was noticed by the UPDF soldiers who were guarding the camp. I heard one of them speak loud in Kiswahili (that I understand but cannot speak fluently), "Sir, I have heard some strange foreign sound." He was ignored and we proceeded to cross another swamp. Still, the soldiers who were not very far from where we were passing heard the sound of the papyrus that was being bent in the process of paving our way. All of a sudden, the whole camp that was in a noisy state was silenced. My colleagues told me to wait on this dangerous side of the camp while they paved way for me, which I did not refuse. I took a ten-litre jerrycan and waited. Again I realised that this was another plan of deserting me in danger, so I carefully followed the trail that they had created through the papyrus swamp and found them waiting for another girl who had gotten stuck in the swamp.

When they saw me approaching, they were not happy as I was back to them with my noise. I ignored their reactions and followed them in silence. Kipindi warned to make sure my baby did not cry as we were not very far from the main road. For three hours in the dark, we followed a murram road with rough stones that I had a hard time walking on because I was used to wearing shoes, the soles of my feet developed painful blisters from small stones. We moved until dawn when Kipindi, who was taking the lead, branched into the bush, passing through tall, thick grass that was dripping from the night's dew.

He lit a fire and we all sat around it warming ourselves, as one girl roasted beans for us to eat. This situation was one that I will always remember. I was feeling extremely cold and had nothing to cover myself with except for a green piece of cloth that I was using to tie my baby with on my back. I shivered from cold, felt hungry, and badly wanted to just take a sip of water but there was not a single drop. Besides that, I was extremely tired. After being given a handful of roasted beans to eat, I placed my head against a tree to rest for thirty minutes before continuing with the journey to where Kipindi told us there was food in abundance.

We started moving around 7 am with a lot of expectation for adequate food to fill our empty stomachs, but this 'promised land' was too far away to be reached at the time we wanted. My colleagues kept insisting on my being hidden in the forest but I completely refused to be left alone in that place (Lomogi), where the locals were known to be hostile, according to a story I had been told earlier. On the way, at around 11 am, we started finding peels and pieces of sugar cane that had been eaten by some people along a pronounced trail that we were following. We picked alot of them and ate since we were starving. My hope for getting enough to eat rose. Little did I know that my colleagues had another plan to desert me that day.

**Abandoned**

A meal of boiled beans was prepared that afternoon and as usual, I was sent to my hiding place with my noisy daughter. But this time I was taken deep into the forest where I sunbathed to warm myself and spread in the sun my daughter's only piece of cloth that had gotten wet in the morning. My portion of the meal was served and my daughter's for her supper, as well. That afternoon, we moved for only one hour and reached a newly ploughed farm that contained vegetables but continued moving until we got a *shamba* of beans. After exploring the area and finding that the security of the place was good, I was told to remain under the shade with my baby where I could control her noise because the sun was too hot, while the four of them picked fresh beans from somebody's *shamba*. Because there was a foot path that was followed by the locals of that area near where I was, I was convinced that this time they were not going to leave me behind. I sat from 2 pm up to 6 pm waiting to be called but nobody came. I cursed myself for accepting to remain and lamented while moving up and down. But it did not make any difference because they were gone and gone forever.

I had left the bunch of bananas that I had cut behind and tried to trace them in vain. I was scared of being left alone because I heard that those who lived in that area were known to kill whoever was escaping from the LRA in revenge for what the LRA had done to them. As I began to move in the direction we had come from, I met someone who ran away when he saw me since both of us were afraid of each other. I also retreated and hid somewhere waiting to see if the person would come with soldiers or anyone to harm me but nobody showed up. I stayed until it got dark and went back to the *shamba* to spend my sorrowful night. I gathered some leaves, spread them on the ground and picked the green piece of cloth that I was using both for tying my baby on my back and as a camouflage so that I could hide from aircraft. I put it down for my baby to lie on but there were lots of mosquitoes that bit us mercilessly. All I thought of at that moment was my life and our safety. I slept until morning, but I asked God what I should do next because I was afraid and confused at the same time. If the rebels found me, they would accuse me of escaping and kill me. If the government soldiers found me, they too would probably kill me or do anything nasty, so I got up. My daughter and I were hungry and I had no breast milk as I had not eaten any food the previous evening, so I sneaked into a garden nearby to uproot cassava. However, this cassava was *akeca* (the type of cassava used only for making local brew called *lujutu)* and therefore too bitter for human consumption when in its raw form. I gave it to her to eat raw while I ate the remaining portion. This kept her quiet as I planned what to do next.

I started moving towards the east on a very bright morning but got wet from the early morning dew that had condensed on the thick grass along the narrow footpath. I decided to turn west since Kipindi had told me there were sugar cane plantations nearby. As far as I knew, sugar cane plantations are often located in swampy areas in valleys and this was what made me change my mind. There was a lot of grass on the footpath, and so I became wet, but I was determined to move ahead. I continued and found a newly planted cassava garden and then after that a groundnuts plantation that had been harvested. All these were signs that human beings were living there. I continued and found an *alup*, a small temporary hut that under normal settings was used by soldiers who were mobile. During war it was used by people as their secret hiding place where they thought the rebels could not reach. I entered after failing to see anybody because I badly needed something to eat. I found fire, and I picked a short piece of wood from the fire, maize flour and water in a jerrycan. I also exchanged their smaller jerrycan of water with mine. One of the precious things that I also picked was salt then I went and sat near their garden, lit a fire, made porridge. This gave me some energy to start my journey again.

I also took away one of their saucepans as well, and decided to go back to where I had been left, thinking that my colleagues might come back for me after having second thoughts. I went right back to where I had slept the previous night and found a good position in a nearby bush for security purposes. Near to where I was, there was a garden that consisted of a variety of crops like pigeon peas, beans, and okra. I picked some of the okra and cooked it then I decided to stay there until my colleagues found me. Unfortunately it rained and and the fire was put out. To protect my baby's only piece of cloth from getting wet, I put it in a polythene bag and sat on it.

It rained on me for nearly thirty minutes and we shivered terribly. My baby looked straight in my eyes and I felt she was communicating to me to do something to stop the suffering. I thought to myself, "If this child also dies due to cold like the first one who was hit by a bomb then life will be useless for me. All that I have gone through in Uganda was for these kids." I had no way out. If I moved on, some unkind person would maybe get me and slaughter me, so my mind was mixed up.

That evening after it had stopped raining, I went back to the home where I had earlier on picked items. The family members were already home, and I could hear them complain, "Someone has taken our saucepan. The person must be having a bad motive." There were three women, one man and a child, from what I heard. They thought it was a thief who had taken their property. I then moved about their home, through the bush to dodge them in the hope of continuing my journey to a place I was not yet sure of.

When I reached a well-cleared *shamba* that was close by their home, I removed my gumboots so as to cross the field without being noticed, but when I heard them talking from the direction I had come from, I branched off and hid in the tall spear grass that was at a boundary and watched them. I heard them talking about the stolen items and got scared in case they noticed me, as I was even carrying them (the saucepan and the jerrycan). I was praying to my dear God for my child not to utter any sound so we wouldn't be noticed. The two women who had probably come to help the man and his wife bid them good-bye and left the couple and their child. The ladies went to the direction that I was heading, so I changed my direction for safety.

I passed through the garden and went back to pick only one log that contained fire from the couple's home, then headed towards a papyrus swamp. I moved across a garden to avoid being noticed and went to the far end of the garden with the hope of camping there because it was a little dry, until I found a better solution to my situation.

I lit a fire to warm myself and stayed there but after three days, the family got scared and left as I could no longer hear their baby crying. Each day I would wake up, pick fresh beans from a nearby garden and cook them, then move around in the afternoons searching for civilians, so that I could explain my case to them and ask for their help to bring me back home without passing through soldiers. I was determined to find a road that led me out of where I was. I also thought that if I heard gun shots, I would know that the LRA was on one side and the UPDF on the other side. But again, if the LRA found me here they would think I was escaping and they would kill me. And on the other side if the UPDF found me, it would also mean trouble. I kept on moving every other day with the hope of finding a church mission or civilians but not the antagonising armed groups. I would move from 1pm to 3 pm then go back to my original position after failing to trace the people I needed for help. My other thought was that if the fire went off, I would have nowhere to get it from since my unknown host had left already, and as far as I knew, nobody else lived there. Instead, they commuted from the IDP camps to work on their farms. Moreover, in my every attempt I always found myself in the same place even if I took other routes (the same *alup* where the owners had fled).

On the fifth day, it rained heavily in the night, and the fire that I used for cooking and warming myself in the night was put out. I wondered how I was going to survive because the family had also shifted. I got up and put my baby on my back and said, "If today is my day for either dying or surviving, then here I am Lord. Do as you wish for my life is in your hands."

I also packed five mushrooms that I had preserved by roasting two days earlier. The way I got the mushrooms was like a miracle to me because when I reached the anthill where they were growing, I felt like something within me was telling me to move ahead, up to the anthill. There I found the three big, white mushrooms and two other smaller ones. This gave me a lot of joy, as it was one of my favorite dishes. I hurried with a lot of excitement, uprooted and prepared some for myself to enjoy. That was how I changed my diet when I was alone in the jungle. I put the remaining roasted mushrooms together with the saucepan on my head and started moving.

## Rescued at last

I moved to that nearby home where I had picked items and met the man and his wife who were just arriving from the camp where they had fled. When he saw me, he was scared just like I was but I was the first to speak saying "I have been left behind by the LRA. I have stayed here for a week now." He said, "You mean you have been staying here all along in the rain?" I began to explain to them how I reached there and who I am. He said, "You are suffering and yet people who have returned from the bush are well off now. One top commander John is always telling his wife called *Min Ogen* (mother of Ogen) to come back home. I will take you, and you will even live a better life than I am living now." I then introduced myself to him as the Min Ogen he had heard a lot about. He got excited and offered to take me to the UPDF soldiers. This I accepted on two conditions. First of all, I wanted to get back home to my people that I had left eight years back and secondly, I needed his assurance that the UPDF were not going to do anything to harm me.

He got his bicycle and gave it to another man who we met on the way to go ahead and inform the UPDF soldiers who were about to leave their current location to another detach to wait until I reached so that they could transport me too towards the town. In my heart, I was filled with a lot of shame that my body could not express because of the way I looked. I was tiny with a big belly, dressed in my only old, pleated, black skirt and a brown blouse that was spotted with blue flowers, with a patch that I made on my arm after it was burnt. My hair was uneven. In the middle of my head, there was no hair because of carrying loads.

On our way to the army detach, my new friend updated me on what had happened that made him flee his *alup* after realising that some of his household items were missing and how soldiers were sent to look for me by setting ambushes. They would come in and lay an ambush in the morning. As for me, I used to move in the afternoon when they had left. He told me that the civilians were set up in that village to pick those who returned home from the bush, and they were paid for this service so this assured me of my safety. Even soldiers were good. They would not harm anyone returning from the bush after being briefed. That is what gave me the courage.

He then took me to soldiers at Labongo Ogali Army Detach. We met some UPDF soldiers on the way and they fired bullets to the direction from which we were coming, and I was scared that they would shoot me. They told me they were doing that to scare away LRA if they were there as we were about to reach their detach. They wanted me to use another short cut route in the bush, however I refused as I feared they may have a bad motive against me, so I opted for the main road. We met their leader who introduced himself to me as a captain in charge of that unit of soldiers. He also asked me if I had a gun and how many people were in the bush. I told him how I had managed to survive alone after being abandoned. At first they could not believe me, but later on they did. He was the one who told me that it was the group under his command whose ambush we had entered. He mentioned names of people I knew like my co-wife so it was clear he was telling the truth. I felt so sad that those I got to know in suffering had lost their lives and I would miss them forever in this life.

The soldiers made some porridge and then food for me to eat, I felt as if I was daydreaming at the sight of the porridge made out of fine, white maize flour. It had been eight years since I had taken it. An army truck came to transfer soldiers from that detach, and that's how I got to be in Labongo Ogali Army Detach. I stayed there for three days waiting for a truck to transport me to Gulu, so that I could trace my home. While in transit, I was the only female in that truck. This scared me a lot as some of the soldiers were drunk, and they kept throwing nasty comments about the rebels to me. Others were even punching their friends. One in particular was given a blow in the face, and he started bleeding right away. It was not a very good journey, but I reached Labongo Ogali Detach safely and I was handed over to the officer in charge. The army commander in this new detach bought my daughter a dress because she was naked and fed me well for the three days that I spent there. I would spend my nights in a special *adaki* that had been sheltered and had a locally made bed in the hole. I was given a blanket to use but it felt so strange though nice to sleep in a sheltered place and moreover covered in a new blanket. I felt good and happy, and at last I started to have hope of surviving, though I had not yet reached my real home. My sleeping place was warm because for nearly two weeks I had been sleeping in the cold without anything to cover my body. I could not believe that some UPDF soldiers were that kind.

On arrival in Gulu town, I was dropped at the main army barracks where some kind of registration was done. I was told to give my particulars then shown to a place by one soldier who told me something that scared me a lot. He showed me a very big scar on one of his arms. He had been wounded when they were sent to rescue the girls abducted from my school in 1996. This scared me and I opened my mouth in surprise because I thought he had the motive of revenging or doing something to harm me as I was in their barracks, but that was not the case. This made me remember the first serious exchange of fire that took place on the second day of our abduction where we were held at gunpoint until the fighting was over.

The next morning my dad who was working in Gulu, came to see me. On seeing me, he burst into a loud cry, and I wondered why he was doing so. I was the one who gave him courage not to shed any more tears because I was there, alive though traumatised, shabby, and in tatters with a bald head, carrying a malnourished toddler.

He later narrated to me that he had bought the *New Vision* newspaper that morning when he was going to work and placed it on his office desk, leaned on the desk and started weeping, saying, "People's children are coming back but mine is not. Why not?" Someone then called him on phone from Lira and told him, "Grace has returned. She is in the papers." He then read the paper and began to look for me.

I reunited with my family at the beginning of September 2004 in the afternoon. I was so eager to see my people. My brother who follows me came to open the gate to let us in, and he looked grown up already. I found very many people waiting to see me alive after receiving a message from those who survived the July 17th attack that I had been shot dead together with my son, Ogen.

My mother ran, hugged me and wept bitterly but still, I wondered what she was crying for. I was so strong-hearted and grateful for my life. They were sympathising with my appearance. I reflected on the dangerous situations that I had gone through, including one where I slept alone in a game reserve and an animal came in the night when I was asleep, but was scared away by the fire that I had lit to give me warmth. I concluded that they had no reason to cry after seeing me alive though in a bad condition. Despite my condition, I could fluently speak all the three languages that I knew before and recognised all I knew before. Many people, including friends and relatives, came one after the other for more than a month to see me and hear how I had survived. Consequently, I would talk a lot until I decided to hide away from people in order to rest from narrating bush stories.

# 15

## Life after captivity

*"I really wanted to go back to school irrespective of my age..."*

I stayed at home without being taken to any counseling centre for about one month, and thereafter I was asked by one of my former classmates, who was then a lawyer, to help him and work as a pay phone attendant. My answer to his request was positive, as I waited for the beginning of the next academic year, since that would have saved me the burden of narrating my bush stories to those who came to visit me. I did simple calculations when changing money for customers and this enabled me to notice the new changes that had taken place in town in my absence. This increased my desire to join school again, this had been my ambition even when I was still in the bush. I really wanted to go back to school irrespective of my age because I had put it clearly in my mind that what happened to me was beyond my control.

Having stayed out of school for eight good years, I doubted my ability to compete effectively with other students, so I decided to start from senior two instead of senior three.

This was a difficult decision to make after seeing my former classmates that I used to teach ahead of me and already working. I picked up courage and said to myself, "If others can, why not me? I will not mind whatever people will say about my past, age or appearance, so long as I can grasp what the teacher is teaching and pass to the next class." With these words, I went to Kampala for the first time to look for a school, together with my five friends who had been abducted from Aboke girls. They also wanted to continue with their studies, and we were all admitted in the same school.

I was delighted when I received my admission letter and instantly started preparing to go to school. I recieved a sponsorship from a rehabilitation center that was started in memory of Sr. Rachele. The first thing I did was to start purchasing items like long slit-less skirts, white pairs of socks, and many others. My only worry was my fourteen month- old toddler, and how she would miss me. My consolation dwelt on the importance of education, which was one of the ways of preparing for our future, and I went to school with a lot of enthusiasm to study without wasting a single minute, to compensate for the lost years.

We went as a group of six formerly-abducted young women. We were cleared then given a room, where we laid our beds and then went out of the hostel to the kitchen at around 7 pm to ask for supper. When the school warden saw us at the wrong time, he asked, "Where are you people from?" One of us responded that we were from home. His response was nasty when he heard that. He was like, "Are you from the bush?" This annoyed us, though we played it cool.

The next day we woke up as early as 4 am to prepare ourselves for classes. We crossed from the boarding section to the day section that was just a few meters away at 6 am. The normal lessons started at 8am, then we had a twenty minute break from 10.40 am to 11 am. Lunch break was from 1 pm to 2 pm, then classes ended at 4 pm. Thereafter, we went back to the boarding section where we resided. This was not as easy as we thought because my friends and I kept on facing challenges like waking up earlier than usual, copying notes that were completely different from the ones we had used eight years ago, relating with students who were much younger and had not undergone the experience we went through. Generally, we found difficulty in getting used to the school environment. My new class had the naughtiest students in the whole school. These were students, especially boys, who would boo at any non-class members and tease fellow classmates. This made other students fear them, but I was not afraid of any of them.

On the first day when we entered the class, one thin and short boy called Sam came with a piece of paper and asked that I write my name. I wrote it, but later another boy again asked me to write my name. This time I realised they were only making fun of me, so I ignored him. All I did was to concentrate on what the teachers taught, and analyse it well to judge whether academically I was still capable of learning. After two weeks, our biology teacher gave us a test, and I was the second best. This result gave me a lot of courage and I said to myself, "If I can defeat these young boys and girls with fresh brains then I am capable of performing." So I continued reading my notes and paying attention to my teachers. Whenever my class was noisy, I would still continue to read, although I faced challenges in other subjects like French, Music, Moral Education, and Fine Art. Out of the seventeen subjects that I was taking, these gave me a hard time at first.

One day our class made a lot of noise and the teacher on duty called everyone out at around 10 am, and he administered four strokes of the cane on our buttocks. This was a bitter pill to swallow, as it reminded me of the beatings that occurred to me while in the bush. This annoyed me to an extent that I nearly gave up on my studies, because of the pain that reminded me of the past. Frankly speaking, I was not a participant of the noise making and yet I was punished because of the few who did it. Nevertheless, life went on, and I managed to finish that whole year with encouraging results that gave me a lot of hope in education. At times when I failed subjects like Mathematics I would feel bad and lament that my life would have been different had it not been for the abduction. My roommates and 'sisters' kept on encouraging me to forget about the past and look ahead to the future.

One day when I was still in senior two, our English language teacher misplaced her book, and she came asking in class for whoever had seen it. The response was not clear, so she decided to punish the whole class just because our class monitor refused to answer her. She ordered the whole class to get out to be punished. On hearing this and remembering how painful canings were, I got up to speak and defend the whole class. I said, "Teacher, how can we all be punished just because our class monitor doesn't know his duties?" I was very serious when speaking so the teacher excused us. From then on my classmates, especially the stubborn boys, began calling me Iron Lady Cecilia Ogwal, referring to the woman member of parliament from my home district, who was very tough and spoke without fear.

The next year I was promoted to senior three, the class I had been in before my abduction. I had dropped seven subjects and was specialising in ten, which I was to sit for my Ordinary Level Certificate. I campaigned for a leadership post and was elected as the Assistant Head Girl. This raised my hope, and I served diligently since they trusted me to lead them. One thing I learnt about leadership is that when you do what you are expected to do as a leader, like being transparent, you will always be given the respect you deserve, and if you are not found in the wrong, then you will definitely excel as a leader. I learnt these lessons from the past mistakes of the leaders before me, and I assured my fellow students during my open campaign period that I would deliver my promises. Indeed, that was what I did. From then on, very many students from all classes became my friends and life became easy for me. Others saw what I was doing as a hindrance to their freedom because I was very strict when it came to following school rules and orders. What I did was to make sure that I followed the rules and implemented them I wanted to be a role model to those I was leading.

By the time I was in senior four, almost the whole class was friendly to me. Nobody amongst them wanted to see me sad. When I entered class and I was moody, I would hear all sorts of comments like, "Acan, don't even enter if you are still wearing that gloomy face." Another would say, "Acan, do you know what you look like when you are in such a mood?" All these plus others and the leadership training that I got when I was elected a prefect made me change my ways of relating to people of all characters. I was someone who was too serious to be befriended. I thought this was the best way of keeping me away from things that distract me from my studies but I was wrong. It did keep them away but it also attracted many more who wanted to discover what kind of person I was. Mostly the naughty boys of my class did this. When they discovered that I was approachable, they became my friends but with a limit, meaning they were very cautious on whatever they said to me.

## Studying amidst Challenges

Back at home, I was always worried about how my daughter was doing. One time when I came for holidays, I found that the babysitter had burnt her arm with a flat iron. This made me very angry, but I kept quiet because I could not help the situation for I was always away.

Another incident also occurred whereby my step-sister and my step-mother's granddaughter came to visit us in my absence and the way she treated my daughter was not right as I was told. She isolated her and said that she was sick, because of her small body size. She locked her in a room and instructed her not to come out, as she would contaminate my step-mother's granddaughter. This caused me a lot of pain and I wanted to confront my step-sister but I chose to calm down. I told my brother about how my daughter was being treated and my plan of leaving school to come and take care of her. His response was that my remaining at home would not solve the problem. By staying in school, I would be working to overcome future problems that would face both my daughter and me.

To add to that, whenever I came back from school, I found find some of my things like clothes or even sandals missing. They were either given away to relatives in my absence without my knowledge or stolen by maids. Whenever I asked about them, I never got a clear answer even after I had packed them properly before leaving for school and it had been so difficult for me to acquire them. All this added to my sorrow.

On two occasions when I was away, my younger sister and my daughter reported to me that a relative had made a very nasty comment and said that my daughter was ill-mannered and that I was the one teaching her bad manners. This made me wonder how exactly I was doing that. I asked myself, "How can I hate my own daughter even if everyone is against her for some reason that I cannot explain?" This made my daughter so scared of my relative. To confirm this, I went to visit my people one time and found my daughter with a wound on one of her cheeks. She had been pinched by my relative just because she was afraid of him or her. My question was, "How can someone fail to fear someone who is ever shouting and blaming you?" I felt like on certain occasions my daughter and I were discriminated against, and it pains me to this day. The only joy that I got when I went home was that of seeing my daughter. After one year, I came and found that my daughter had been taught to call me by my name. Although she did that, she realised the difference between the love and care I gave to her and she began calling me 'Mum' without me reminding her, and my mother complained that I was the one who had taught her to call me 'Mum'. I did not quite understand why she had a problem with my child addressing me as mother.

# 16

## Conclusion

*"Always get up and move on..."*

I kept on working hard at school to change my life, and when I sat for my Ordinary Level Certificate, I got a first grade that qualified me to join advanced level. This made me feel joyous as I was progressing in my studies, although I was facing problems in terms of school requirements because no one from home was able to assist me.

When I was in senior four, I wanted to do a science course because I truly loved Biology as a subject. On several occasions I had been the best in my class in that subject, and whenever the subject was being taught, I grasped it right away from the teacher's explanation because it mainly explained functions of the human body. When I sat for the ordinary certificate, however, things did not turn out well, though I passed with a first grade. I performed well in arts subjects instead, so I decided to forget about sciences and went for Arts.

When I went back to the same school for my advanced level, most students who had been satisfied with my leadership as a prefect were so happy to see me back, and they encouraged me to contest again as the their head girl. This was not a very easy decision to make since I had experienced how difficult it was to be a leader. I was finding it tough to adjust to the new level in terms of questions and approach in class. It involved a lot of sacrifice and I needed to concentrate in order to pass. On the other hand, a leader is respected and has some privileges. I decided to contest for the post of headgirl

It was not easy to balance both books with leadership and the stress that one goes through before they are qualified during campaign. It first involved campaigning and convincing the whole school from class to class. Then there was an open campaign where the short-listed candidates made themselves known to the school and convinced the students to elect them. Thereafter, elections were conducted and the winners were declared then sworn in as prefects. All these were stressing processes as they involved various reactions from the students which could either be positive or negative. I was elected for the second time, and became head girl.

I studied for five years in the same school and left after sitting for my Advanced Level Certificate but had no hope for further studies because the organisation that was sponsoring us abruptly stopped sponsoring students who intend to join university.

However, my results came back, and I got all the four principle passes that were required for one to join university and I had the previledge of joining Gulu University for a degree course in development studies.

In May 2013, it was my greatest pleasure to complete my studies like others had done! I hope in future to continue with my studies at a graduate level. I am now married and have two children, who love my eldest daughter so much.

In the time I have spent on earth, I have learnt that life is not smooth. It is full of ups and downs but what matters is how you perceive it and move on. No matter how many troubles you go through or how many times you fall, always get up and move on as that won't be the end of the journey.

# Glossary

| | |
|---|---|
| **adaki** | Trenches dug all around the perimeter of an army barracks that were used for hiding in case of an attack |
| **apwap** | A place located on an isolated mountain slope. |
| **adyebo** | wild plants |
| **akeca** | the type of cassava used only for making local brew |
| **alup** | a small temporary hut |
| **anyaka** | girl (in Lwo) |
| **boo** | green vegetables |
| **dura** | flour like sorghum that is used to prepare bread |
| **kado atwona** | local salt |
| **lapena** | pigeon peas |
| **lapwony** | teacher |
| **lugwiri/coroko** | small green peas |
| **lujutu** | local brew |
| **mony pa Kony** | child soldiers below fourteen years of age |
| **moo yao** | shea nut oil |
| **ngwen** | white ants paste |
| **nyakidi** | stones used for grinding millet |
| **nyoi** | a meal of boiled beans mixed with maize |
| **okurut** | recruits |

| | |
|---|---|
| **olalu** | a name used to refer to Ugandan government soldiers (Uganda People's Defence Forces-UPDF) |
| **otigolwoka** | okra |
| **posho** | cornbread made from ground maize flour |
| **shamba** | a field used for growing crops |
| **tania** | a Sudanese snack made from sesame (sim-sim) and sugar |
| **wir** | cleansing/initiation |